# Beyond the
# ICARUS
# FACTOR

# Beyond the
# ICARUS
# FACTOR

## Releasing the
## Free Spirit of Boys

RICHARD HAWLEY, Ph.D.

Park Street Press
Rochester, Vermont

Park Street Press
One Park Street
Rochester, Vermont 05767
www.ParkStPress.com

Park Street Press is a division of Inner Traditions International

**The Library of Congress Cataloging-in-Publication Data**
Hawley, Richard.
  Beyond the Icarus factor : releasing the free spirit of boys / Richard Hawley.
    p. cm.
  Includes bibliographical references and index.
  ISBN-13: 978-1-59477-228-3 (pbk.)
  ISBN-10: 1-59477-228-2 (pbk.)
  1. Boys—Psychology. 2. Spontaneity (Personality trait) 3. Creative ability in children.
4. Maturation (Psychology) 5. Conformity. I. Title. II. Title: Releasing the free spirit of boys.
  HQ775.H39 2008
  155.43'2—dc22

                 2007045609

Printed and bound in the United States at Lake Book Manufacturing

10  9  8  7  6  5  4  3  2  1

Text design and layout by Priscilla Baker
This book was typeset in Garamond, with Basilea and Legacy Sans used as display typefaces

To send correspondence to the author of this book, mail a first-class letter to the author c/o Inner Traditions • Bear & Company, One Park Street, Rochester, VT 05767, and we will forward the communication.

# CONTENTS

"Save him, save him!" cried Wendy looking with horror at the cruel sea far below. Eventually Peter would dive through the air, and catch Michael just before he could strike the sea, and it was lovely the way he did it, and you felt it was his cleverness that interested him and not the saving of human life.

—J. M. BARRIE, *PETER PAN*

# PROLOGUE

THE OBSERVATIONS AND arguments posed in this book are based on a single, urgent assumption: that we have created a culture that cannot by its very nature understand children and nurture them to their full realization. We have arrived at this condition through no lack of journalistic or therapeutic attention to the "problem." Indeed the proliferation of analysis and proposed remedies for the various ways in which children are failing to thrive is symptomatic of what is wrong. For more than a decade there has been a mounting tide of mass market books devoted to imperiled children, to newly noted pathologies and dysfunctions, to therapeutic strategies. Headlines and cover stories in newspapers and news weeklies are full of sensational claims about children's declining scholastic competence and the rising incidence of addictions, illnesses, and antisocial behavior.

A common feature to these alarming reports is that they carry with them no promise of remedy or improvement, nor do they deliver any. There is a reason for this, a reason common to all rampant, seemingly ubiquitous social problems that defy solution—and that is that the analysts and pundits are thinking *with*, not *about*, the assumptions that are causing the problem. At the heart of this increasingly normative inability to understand children is that their putative "problems" and "crises" are seen and reflexively responded to as failures of children to articulate smoothly into the established cultural order. What is proposed here is an invitation to look at children and the culture in which they are embedded in a different way. Although seemingly simple, this invitation to reconsider and reorient ourselves to children is radical in its implications. It requires beginning with a loving and attentive witness to children—to what they are like and to how their experiences unfold. We must undertake this witness of children prior to and independently of any cultural expectations and designs on them. It is proposed here that our collective problem is not that children are failing to serve the culture, but that the culture is failing to serve children—failing even to acknowledge the most elemental things about them.

A world good for and fit for children may indeed be the world most worth having generally. Contemporary children, however, even those who dwell in the most technologically advanced and economically prosperous societies, cannot be said to be thriving. It has long been normative, first among psychologists and now generally, to consider coming of age a "crisis." More recently there are suggestions that the crisis has devolved into a widespread and mounting failure to educate and socialize children effectively. The concern is no longer merely that they succeed in school and make transitions to adult productivity. The more immediate concern is that children will thrive at all, that they will endure a school day, with or without the intervention of powerful psychoactive medicines. There is concern that they will lapse into debilitating depression or incapacitating anxiety, that they will become addicted to drugs or alcohol or be drawn into the thralldom of gang rituals and violence, that they will starve themselves past recovery, that they will take their lives or the lives of others.

Children's failure to thrive is increasingly normative. Titles of bestselling books about children suggest that to raise a daughter requires "reviving Ophelia," while rearing a son is "raising Cain." Ophelia is a suicide, Cain a fratricide. The older child or emerging adolescent in contemporary fiction and films is no longer seen as facing a challenging or even perilous world, but a world spoiled beyond redemption. The young hero is an antihero. It is a world in which a rebel could not conceivably locate a cause. It is a world in which a child might age but not mature. *The world that created me deserves me,* pledge the young terrorists of Columbine, the defiant misogynists of gangsta rap. The youthful antihero is no longer J. D. Salinger's Holden Caulfield, melancholy and adrift in midtown Manhattan. Holden is a lost boy, but he is lost longingly among ghosts of golden times and golden comrades from his earlier childhood. Today's lost boys long for nothing; indeed they have known nothing one would long for.

The contemporary boy, the contemporary son, is not so much lost as broken. A reading of the historical and cultural record will reveal, perhaps surprisingly, that he has been lost for a long time. The broken boy, by contrast, is a genuine novelty. Where did he come from? How does he come to be? Is there repair, a way forward, a return?

# 1  🍥

# THE EXPERIENCE OF BOYS

## SCHOOL: AN ILLUSION

For years I have been the headmaster of a school for boys. If you enter the building on any given morning you will see a whirl of purposeful activity as hundreds of high-school boys stream into Morning Assembly to the hurrying cadence of amplified music, a rousing trumpet voluntary. The boys wear blue blazers, school ties, and khaki pants. Some of them look tousled and disheveled as they approach the auditorium. As they near the entrances, which are attended by faculty members, the boys may adjust the knots of their ties so that they rest properly in the V of their shirt collars. Crisp but friendly greetings are exchanged as the boys enter.

Inside, the music is muted until the hall is quiet. The boys attend to the morning's business: announcements of many activities and meetings, the reporting of the teams' scores from the previous day. Then perhaps one of the seniors might deliver his required Senior Speech, or a guest speaker might address a topical issue. Occasionally, I speak to the assembled school about a disciplinary matter or some other school concern.

After assembly the boys file out, stopping at their lockers. Some shed their ties and jackets; others keep them on. They make their way up the great central staircase to classes, laboratories, the library. Those without a first period class head off to the student commons where they finish homework, review for tests, chat with friends. Some go instead to the new fitness center where they remove their shoes and lift weights.

The classes themselves are outwardly casual but quickly get down to business. With few extraneous gestures and little resistance, the boys are soon translating Latin lines, answering questions in Spanish or French, solving equations at the chalkboard, and negotiating their way through computer software that enables them to design buildings or to animate images. In studios, pots are thrown. In the darkroom, images are coaxed into definition. Walking the bright corridor of the humanities wing, you would hear loud faculty voices stressing the conventions of the sonnet, the progression of ancient battles, the distinction between skepticism and non-belief.

At midmorning the boys break for snacks—donuts, bagels—or to attend the dozens of organizational meetings announced earlier. At lunchtime they dine in clusters of six or seven—"family style"—with an attending faculty member. Afternoon classes are followed for most boys by team practices and outdoor activities like cycling, casual tennis, kayaking, or trailblazing in the woodlands surrounding the school. In the evening some of them return for drama and choral rehearsals, review courses for standardized tests, or work on school publications: the literary magazine, newspaper, yearbook. Before they retire for the night, the boys will find a way to dispatch two or three hours of homework. It is, for all of us, a long, full day.

It is difficult, after so many years, for me to summarize a typical school day without an almost wearying awareness of its orderliness. There is so much forward motion as we move from bell to bell, class to class, meeting to meeting, event to event. The familiarity and continuity of such days tend to dull our awareness of what, if we were not bound together in school, might occur to us as bracing and discontinuous. We only faintly sense, for example, the changing of seasons, mark them less by their distinctive natural manifestations than by the routines we impose upon them: a new season of sport, another grading period. Nor, really, do we take much note of an even more immediate drama: that the boys in our charge are changing and growing. They are, yearly, outgrowing school, but this is never acknowledged, and even the boys themselves fail to take notice. Their change and growth are presumed in the orderly succession of freshman, sophomore, junior, and senior status. When the seniors matriculate on to their various universities in June, they do not seem at all lost to us, for in the fall we will have seniors once more.

Not that we do not regard our graduates fondly. We feel we have taught and tamed them, exercised and enjoyed them. They carry with them, we believe, the mark of their time with us. We understand they will progress through the expected next stage in their personal unfolding. They will proceed through their higher education, and then they will enter the professions, take their adult positions in commerce. We will keep track of them. Those who return to the city to live and work will very likely send us their sons.

There is something undeniably reassuring about the continuity in the careers of the boys who pass through my school. This is the way, we come to accept, it is supposed to be. It is the way the world works.

Of course we do not mean this literally. Most of the peoples on the planet know no such scholastic or vocational or civic continuity. We mean, rather, that this is the way *our* world works, admittedly (even smugly) a small world, but a world that works, as surely as bell follows bell, as juniors follow seniors.

And if we step back to gain a much broader, more comprehensive view, don't we see a world, in this case a nation, that works? At the level of village or national polity, laws are made and enforced. Magistrates succeed magistrates in a peaceful, orderly way. Successive generations assume necessary roles in the economic and domestic orders. Yes, there is chafing in the interstices. There is ferment. There is creativity. There is progress. But above all, there is an unmistakable order—as orderly, a moment of reflection might reveal, as a school day or year.

Last spring as I was conferring prizes on the school's annual Prize Day, it occurred to me with considerable pleasure that I had taught the fathers of most of the boys receiving awards. The sons were quite similar to their fathers, but by no means identical. One would be more happy-go-lucky than his grim, rather driven father. Another would be more fastidious, another funnier, another dreamier than his father. But they were unmistakably, in the cowlick and in the chin, their father's sons. At that moment, conferring those prizes, I experienced a profound sense of continuity at work in the world. For that moment it occurred to me that all change, creativity, and novelty were held fast in a gentle dynamic of a greater order. I had watched as those boys' fathers had grown up and out of school and then taken their places in the order of the city. I knew the sons were on their purposeful way.

Or so it seemed. And so it always seems to me whenever I peer out the window of an airplane cabin at night and see below me the vast, twinkling grid work of the city where I live. The pleasing geometries are saved from predictability by quirks and irregularities of topography, but there seems to be no question that a design is at work. Jewel-lit at night, the design is lovely and benign, certainly far more so than the conscious plans any earthbound designer could conceive. The thought is deeply comforting, although my comfort is irrational; I know this city. Enclosed in that glittering grid are housing projects of heartbreaking ugliness. That dazzling spray of gems is only a mall. Those streets, when I come to land, are mean streets.

## SCHOOL: A REALITY

Keeping school requires a kind of compulsory amnesia. What veteran schoolmaster doesn't know in his heart the hopeless elusiveness of continuity and order. There is always just below the hum and crackle of a school day the unnerving suspicion that anything—the worst—could happen. Sometimes it does. A carload of boys full of beer and full of the devil can speed off into the night and never return home. At the precise moment of the collision, they are in a kind of dream state, not fully in the world. Some boys burn to make trouble that no school can contain. Some boys fall into a thrall of hopelessness and sadness they cannot begin to name. Psychiatrists find a name. Medicines are prescribed. But for those boys a black hopelessness threatens to open up before them like an endless beckoning pit. Some boys catch an intimation of paradise or sensual ecstasy and cannot thereafter see the point of slogging through deadening routines, spending themselves in competition, dressing according to occasion, or even simply bending to a standard. Some boys sense the emptiness and capriciousness of standards and decide to test them all, as they might thrust a fist through a cardboard wall. Such boys will assume the manners of a subjugated race. They will grow or remove their hair in an outlandish way. They will stain and pierce their flesh. They will provoke. They will hold maddeningly back. They will take up arms and the uniform of the enemy. Many other boys will not do these things but will locate their own dream state in which they will savor stories of flight and rebellion and listen to thudding, pounding anthems of mayhem through their headsets.

The simple, problematic fact is that no boy passes cheerfully and readily into the civil order of the adult world. Some may seem to—and aren't their parents and teachers proud and relieved—but, as we shall see, such boys are only masquerading, held temporarily in a dream of Conventional Success. They may take their part in this imposture because their personal circumstances have manipulated or intimidated them from realizing themselves and finding their own way. Highly rationalized and effective families, schools, and communities occasionally succeed in obliterating from youth's view any imaginable path of divergence or individuation. Such youths, though in fact severely arrested in their personal unfolding, have all the outer markings of gratifying achievers. They are for a time the prizewinners, celebrated golden boys.

But there is about them, always, a detectable quality of unreality. The very best of them seem vaguely inauthentic, a little too good to be true. Moreover, this hint of inauthenticity becomes more heavily pronounced as the imposture is carried on into adulthood. Despite perhaps impressive passages into good positions and the acquisition of "trophy" spouses and early domestic comforts, the weight of having unconsciously taken up a persona that is no more than a civic dream begins to take its toll. The imposture can only be maintained by the will, with deadening effort. Thus the golden boy becomes brittle, perhaps chronically ill, his social gestures predictable and uninteresting. Such men might be enviably reliable and on that account valuable to their communities, but they are far from happy. The fortunate among them begin to acknowledge their unhappiness. They are good, but good in a way that distances themselves puzzlingly from others. There may be plenty of purposeful activity and social occasion, but there is little connection or release. There is no deep pleasure. Such men meet their commitments, but they cannot find intimacy. As a character in a Flannery O'Connor short story puts it, such men are good, but *right*. As such they are headed for one of two kinds of trouble.

The first kind of trouble is eerily familiar; it is the kind we read about in the papers. The pillar of the community is suddenly, spectacularly disgraced. The President dallies with a bimbo. The rabbi has been accessing the most repellant pornography on his office computer. The lionized coach of perennial state championship teams is caught in a sexual relationship with a player. The youth minister is a pedophile. The chief accountant takes to playing the horses, then cooking the books. Such troubles are always news, and though they strike a deeply resonant note in us, we talk about them as if they are a great surprise. Even more strangely, we can't get enough of such news. But, as we shall see, this kind of trouble is not the worst. As it happens, the inner agents of life-changing Eros or mayhem can be lifesaving. Very often they and the transgressions they inspire serve, in a courageous soul, as the announcement that the imposture is over, its weight too great. Disgrace is, apart from its attendant losses and embarrassments and punishments, an invitation to be born again and to live.

It is, spiritually speaking, far worse trouble to carry on the imposture unto death. To do so unconsciously leads to increasing personal alienation, bitterness, and loneliness. The man who has never grown conscious of his imposture and its costs feels, in his allegiance to lofty standards, betrayed by his era and all others. He tries to love and feel loved by those who admire him, but he can't—because it is his noble imposture, not himself, that is admired. That imposture is a psychic construct, not a self or a soul, formed in late childhood in order to defend the conscious self from the fear of uncertainty and loss of approval. An even more profound despair is visited on the man who becomes consciously aware that his defining qualities are not really his, but a compensation for his youthful fears and boyhood failure to set forth on the uncertain journey of his individuation. This realization— and the judgment that it is too late to attempt the original journey—is perhaps the ultimate despair. Yet men in this condition can be seen everywhere. They are miserably out of sympathy with the age. They know no intimacy or love. They experience no ecstatic release, either in their minds or bodies. Their spouses perhaps accommodate them. Their spirited children turn away from them. Others keep a distance. The conscious awareness of one's own deep, lifelong imposture is hell itself.

## THE ORIGINS OF IMPOSTURE

That the cultural standard for male development—the good boy, the good man—rests on the assumption of a spirit-crippling imposture seems at once an upsetting and extravagant claim. But it may be nonetheless true.

Boys are not born into imposture. It is not "natural." There is no genetic predisposition. Nor, as might be imagined, are infant boys molded to this imposture by their earliest socialization. Little boys, when they acquire sufficient language and experience to become conceptually aware of their identity as males and of their place in family and community, begin to internalize strong impressions of such ideals as Good Boy, Good Man, and Hero. These earliest impressions are not confining or forbidding. The initial figures of Good Man, Good Father, Good Son, and Hero are sheer story, sheer possibility. As such they take their compelling places in developing consciousness alongside such figures as Wise Man, King, Wizard, Trickster, Villain, and Fool. The civic and moral (and thus culturally preferred) figures may in some instances be heavily endorsed by nurturers and early teachers, but educational emphasis does less to shape the youth's personal identity than the inherent appeal of the archetypal figures themselves.

From his earliest capacity to enter into stories until the onset of pubescence, a boy ranges with a thrilling spiritual liberty through a world in which a lively array of male types play out their adventures and vie for his allegiance. This stage of life is the special preserve of what Jungian thought has called *puer* spirit.

> [The *puer* spirit] wanders to spend or to capture, and to ignite, to try its luck, but not with the aim of going home. . . . The *puer* understands little of what is gained by repetition and by consistency, that is by work. . . . These teachings but cripple its winged heels. . . . It is anyway not meant to walk, but to fly.
>
>    . . . The *puer* attitude displays an esthetic point of view: the world as beautiful images or vast scenario. Life becomes literature, an adventure. The *puer* in any complex gives it its drive and drivenness, makes it move too fast and want too much, go too far.[1]

Every boy is held for a time in the thrall of his puer spirit, and a few manage to dwell in this thralldom for the length of their lives. If one were to bracket this period in years, a good estimate for boys in the West would be between ages three and ten, between preschool and the onset of junior high. In those years boys experience their first consciously autonomous explorations. They find opportunities for undirected play. They experience the constellations of their first friendships, first societies. They discover whom they fear and hate. They feel reverence for the heroes of their stories but also reverence—not merely dread—for villains and magi and tricksters. In their games and improvisations they are quite likely to prefer Indians to Cowboys, the Bad Guys to the Good Guys. Whatever the choices and inspirations, it is hard for a loving adult to be overly concerned about such play. The boys are so happily transported, energized, so fully themselves. If not conventionally "good," they are observably *right*. This time of vivid stories being integrated into actual play is a time of great feeling. It is religious in the sense of being charged with reverence and wonder. It is a period characterized by intense longing, including longing for that which seems to be practically impossible, for worlds and galaxies not yet seen and for wondrous worlds and beings forever lost. Outer space and the era of dinosaurs beckon with equal force. These are what Selma Fraiberg calls "magic years" because the membrane between story and waking reality is permeable. The archetypal figures move easily between both worlds. Imaginary friends speak, clasp your hand, run out ahead of you down the path.

Although the archetypal figures can be domineering and very forceful, the boy beholding them is wonderfully free of having to impose himself in this way. Each boy is for a spell of his time completely unentitled, neither (except for the purposes of a specific game or adventure) ruler nor subject, leader nor follower, hero nor villain. In this he is a natural democrat, neither above nor beneath the fray. In this era of the story and puer play, even boys whose personal circumstances are miserably deprived are capable of great optimism and hope.

Boys held fast in their puer spirit are by no means detached, unreal, or ineffective in their practical situations. Because the puer spirit enlivens, such boys bring great energy and presence to their families and to their schools. Moreover, as Erik Erikson maintains, they are capable of great *industry* as they progress through household, neighborhood, school, and community. Looked at closely, this industry is not practical foresight or good sense; it too is a charged story: the romance of creation and material transformation. In prepubescence boys learn, deeply and forever, the enabling skills of learning: reading, writing, arithmetic. They learn skills they will not forget: riding a bicycle, hitting a ball, swimming, hammering nails. Puer-spirited boys are tenacious builders of models, keepers of pets, collectors of coins, cards, stamps, bottles. They are charmed by badges, uniforms, caps. They are glad to be assumed into dens and troops, teams and clubs. They lose themselves recklessly in the work of tunneling under earth or sand. They are great builders of aeries and forts. Fire, too, has its heady Promethean appeal—and it can be trouble. These boys want to ride it, make it go, make it fly, make it go faster. They want to launch it, detonate it, shoot it into the flanks of prey.

Erikson has identified a distinctive form and trajectory to boys' play. He observed it tellingly in the way boys freely play with blocks.

> The most significant difference was the tendency of boys to erect buildings, towers, or streets. The girls tended to use the play table as the interior of a house, with simple, little, or no use of blocks.
>
> High structures, then, were prominent in the configuration of the boys. But the opposite of elevation, i.e., downfall was equally typical for them: ruins or fallen down structures were exclusively found among boys.[2]

He sees what he calls "phallic intrusiveness" in boys' playful approach to surrounding space.

> The ambulatory stage and that of infant genitality add to the inventory of basic social modalities that of "making," first in the sense of "being on the make." There is no simpler, stronger word for it; it suggests pleasure in attack and conquest; in the boy the emphasis remains on phallic-intrusive modes.[3]

There is a powerfully numinous, sacred feeling to the puer world. Even as the boy vividly lives and feels it, he senses it as closed off, unto itself. It is an enchanted world, a secret garden. Often it is experienced as about to be lost. There is the intimation that once really lost, there can be no return. This is the riverbank and meadow of *Wind in the Willows*, the three-acre wood of Christopher Robin and Pooh, the Arthurian Camelot, Robin Hood's Sherwood Forest, the Kingdom of Oz, Peter Pan's Never-Never Land, Alice's Wonderland, Arcadia of the myths. In the great stories there is only magical entry into, and return from, the enchanted world: down a rabbit hole or through a looking glass or a wardrobe. The journey might require a cyclone or ruby slippers or flight through the stars enabled by fairy dust.

In his study of the literature of this enchanted realm, *Secret Gardens*, Humphrey Carpenter suggests that the production of so many of these powerful fictions between the late nineteenth century and the First World War might be due to a mounting collective sense that the pastoral life had been finally and irreversibly overwhelmed by technology, industry, and urbanization. The modern industrial world's triumph of applied science and rationality leaves no earthly place for secret gardens and enchanted woods.

Prepubescent children, however, even those who are familiar and facile with technology and its products, know otherwise. They are instinctively drawn to any suggestion of numinous places and to the figure of the puer, the eternal child. Most prepubescent children navigate without apparent difficulty through both their practical circumstances and in their secret gardens. They are pleased to grow taller and stronger, to master new skills and tasks, but unlike those who study and teach them, they don't themselves feel caught in a progression of "developmental" stages. Unlike the adolescent, who will become conscious that he must integrate his deepest knowing and desire into a highly rationalized scholastic and civic order, the child still in the thrall of puer spirit feels no such urgency or obligation. From his perspective, new and welcome mastery of language and social effectiveness, new pleasures in movement, games, hobbies, or music-making are perfectly continuous with the enchanted realm of his deepest knowing. For him the world and its ways are not an uncomfortable imposition. Every new experience presents a potentially wondrous face of the enchanted world, the only world, the world into which he feels destined to take his soulful place. Because a child in this condition can feel so happy and so complete, he is likely never, in his deepest knowing, to forget it. He will dread the prospect of its loss; grieve over the realization that it is gone.

Nevertheless, happily, puer spirit is lived and felt before it bows before adolescent necessity. The puer-spirited child senses the wonder in each elegant complexity: constellations of stars, the variety of shells on an ocean beach. The puer spirit is drawn to any glimpse of animals in the wild, to the wild itself. The puer spirit seeks passionately to get to the heart of man-made complexities. The puer spirit wants to lift the hood off engines, to pry open watches and clocks to expose the clockwork. There is an urge to penetrate, dismantle, disassemble, and reassemble everything. The exposed wires and felted hammers of a piano are a wonder—as is any stringed instrument in its plush case. To puer spirit, the gleaming convolutions of a trumpet or a saxophone are an irresistible invitation to handle and to play. Tools, sports equipment, fishing gear—anything sharp-bladed or that shoots—are sheer promise to the puer spirit.

There is much joyous exploration and discovery in this world. There is remembered contentment and happiness. Because of the deep, pleasurable sufficiency of the time, preadolescent years are rightly called "the adulthood of childhood."

The onset of pubescence will challenge and ultimately, for most children, shatter the puer world. The budding adolescent feels the encroachment of both profound biological changes in himself as well as a daunting new set of cultural expectations. Between the twelfth and sixteenth year Western children undergo the fastest period of growth and development they will consciously experience. Only the developing embryo and early infant experience more dramatic cell and tissue growth—but, again, not consciously. The adolescent will reach nearly adult stature. He will achieve full sexual potency. He will become capable of a new, higher order of thought: the ability to draw conclusions, predict, and act on the basis of hypothetical, *a priori* assumptions. Preadolescents, too, are capable of the inspired thought. They can "get it right," but they do so from *a posteriori* premises; they reason and act on the basis of what they have seen and done previously. With the increased myelinization and new neural circuitry in the adolescent's brain, he or she can begin to think systematically. Having internalized a given system—say, the United States Constitution or the school's conduct code or a religious cosmology or an understanding of biological health—the adolescent is fully capable of assuming the universality and invariability of that system and then to draw conclusions, to prescribe and modify behavior accordingly.

Adolescents begin to realize their adult capacity to predict and to plan. And while this realization greatly expands one's personal range of action and effectiveness, it also alienates one from the immediacy, the sensory connectedness of preadolescence and the puer spirit. For the emergent theoretical thinker, the theory itself—the system— becomes the ultimate reality. However strongly adherents to scientific method maintain that theory is an aid to knowing, a mere means to test hypotheses, the adolescent theorist knows no Archimedean point outside the theory. Both school and the larger culture help to convince the adolescent that his personal mission now is to construct a theoretical order that defines the world and his place within it. And for such theorists, it is the order, the theory itself that is true; not one's own anomalous, wayward experience. Theory is tested and validated by cognition—with the head—whereas puer spirit validates experience by the force and richness of feeling. For the adolescent, systematic, theoretical thinking not only explains the order of things, it *is* the order of things. Consequently, one's strongest urges and desires, the very ones that propelled the puer-spirited child through his days, are banished to a suspect preserve of irrationality, of "mere" emotion. The maturing adolescent is enjoined in every way to get real, face the facts, put aside childish things. The educated adolescent is systematically schooled to lose heart.

Adolescence can be seen as a process by which the immediacies of true childhood are either repressed, diverted pathologically, or "sublimated" into culturally approved abstractions. Thus, in modern Western adolescence, one is quite likely to feel unworthy of his own life. Since the theory is universal, invariable, and true, "data" that do not fit are either obsessively troubling or suppressed. Consciously and unconsciously, the costs in doubt and suffering are great. Measuring up to a universal standard is feared to be impossible. Among other personal features, the adolescent's body is often found to be dramatically inadequate. Even visibly, measurably slender girls find themselves too fat, and the realization is unlivable. Eating—the very wellspring of daily vitality—is curtailed or reversed in clinically labeled "disorders." Boys cannot get big or strong enough. For many boys there is no limit—not pain, not threat to life—to what they will do to bulk up and harden the armor of their musculature.

In other ways, too, the adolescent body becomes daily a cruel betrayer. Half-dreaded, half-longed for developments like the appearance of beards or breasts arrive without warning—or humiliatingly late. Like Alice in Wonderland, one can find oneself impossibly large in a miniature world, a pygmy in a world of giants. The adolescent is without warning conscious of acrid smells, woundlike blotches of the skin. Beholding himself in the morning mirror, he does not see his face with a pimple on it; he sees a livid mountainous eruption against an anonymous backdrop of face. Waking life becomes a drama of obsessive, invidious comparisons. Even without such diminished bases of confidence, formerly assured and large-hearted adolescents fall prey to inflated posturings. To their physically less favored peers, those less coordinated, those less socially adept, those whose dress or manner of speech or neighborhood or car is determined to be clearly below newly established standards, the emerging adolescent can be witheringly cruel. But the cruelty is not, at its nub, aggressive; it is a defense, at least temporarily, against one's own deep personal dreads. The put-down and the exclusion serve to distance the uncertain adolescent from his worst nightmare.

Here too, families, schools, and communities that may have provided saving stability and nurturance in earlier childhood are apt to intensify an adolescent's unease. Because they are now older and dramatically more adult in appearance, adolescents are enjoined to act like adults, although they have only the accrued experience of childhood to guide them. Performance in school becomes desperately consequential, especially for those whose families expect either maintenance of desirable status or upward mobility. At school earlier pleasures taken in the mastery of tasks, in research and exploration, in finding things out and making things, is now channeled into a framework of graded work and tested measures. Just as the emerging adolescent finds himself ranked in a worryingly important social order, he is also aware of himself as an "A," "B," or perhaps "D" student. Even students quick to master grade-level requirements are aware that certain of their kind are achieving at unreachably high levels—perhaps deemed "gifted and talented," singled out for more rarefied experiences. Musically, artistically, and athletically, too, somebody in school or in town always seems to be distinguishing himself in almost unthinkable ways: reading Proust, winning national competitions, or qualifying for the Olympics. Somebody is always impossibly, unreachably ahead. The romance and exuberance of games and play is eclipsed by the protocols of organized competitive sport. Willing hands don't make the team, are not issued uniforms. There are first-string and second-string, regulars and subs. As in their social and scholastic relations, athletes and would-be athletes come to know, often excruciatingly, just where they stand.

The explicit and implicit imperative to get ahead, exceed oneself, and win insures that most will fail—not utterly, but considerably, at a time when even the smallest social or scholastic failure can feel—and literally be—unendurable.

The relentless gradations in what is expected of adolescents take their own distinctive toll. First homework, then considerable home-work is assigned. Conscientious students, especially, realize at day's end that they can never do enough. Curricula are structured in such a way that each new operation—the subjunctive use of verbs, the geometry of tangents, the history of an era—is immediately and without rest or much reflection succeeded by a new, more complex operation, one that assumes the mastery of what preceded it. To pause or to miss a step is to fail to master the rest of the sequence. To fail at anything—and, more devastatingly, to be *seen* to fail—is more than many adolescents can bear. Thus, simultaneously embattled by inner betrayals and esca-lating external demands, the adolescent seeks respite in a number of familiar escapes.

The first of these is simple regression. Some children on the thresh-old of puberty balk; they refuse to pass through. Often, but not always, these are physically smaller children, slower in some aspect of their psy-chosocial development. They may be also, secretly, the happiest, dream-iest children, those held most in thrall of their puer spirit and most reluctant to forsake it. They seem oblivious when bigger, more out-wardly sophisticated classmates reveal their early sexual stirrings and cross-gender activity. They will not go there. They hold onto, perhaps quite oddly, early forms of play. They continue to fantasize, to pretend. They are especially likely to get lost in video fantasies and computer games, which serve, sometimes darkly and even dangerously, to hold them fast in an alternative world. In school the regressive adolescent can be a genius of passivity and anonymity. He may reveal considerable tested aptitude but only listless delivery or non-delivery. The regressive is often chronically but not seriously ill. He is literally and figuratively absent a great deal. He favors the old things. He may live in books, par-ticularly if they convey him to Middle Earth or into other galaxies. He is likely to prefer home to school—unless concerned parents become oppressively allied with school staff in the effort to figure him out and get him on track; then he is likely to be a cipher. He will not be notably effeminate, nor will he be definitively masculine—whereas girls in the same regressive crisis may define themselves emphatically as tomboys. Adolescent psychologists are apt to see such boys as passive-aggressive, a diagnosis of considerable elegance and descriptive power. No therapies, however, have proved to be effective in "treating" passive-aggression.

If the weight and tension of adolescent emergence can be ducked and lightened by certain regressive refusals, skipping the business altogether holds out hope for similar relief. There is a certain kind of pubescent child, usually one who has succeeded gratifyingly in school and other closely structured activities, who deflects—or at least defers—anxiety by precociously identifying with authoritative adults. Such children will take on the manner of speech, dress, and general deportment of their teachers and other attending grownups. Adults are accomplished. They are in charge, and those who *teach* are the very custodians of knowledge. Thus the precocious identifier is usually an accomplished student, quick to do the extra thing, read more, invest more time in laboratory work, out-of-school research, and projects. The precocious identifier will be temperamentally, if not actually, more an "enforcer" of adult standards and decorum than the adults themselves. These students are teacher-pleasers, to their peers transparently teacher's pets, although teachers may be slow to recognize this since such children behave themselves, respond enthusiastically, do exemplary work. And, truth be told, a high count of practicing teachers may have been such children themselves.

The adult-identified adolescent seeks to be above the abrading and humiliating competition for social status and acceptance. He has an exasperated intolerance for acting out, anarchic humor, rebellion, and disruption. He would like his peers, in and outside of school, to grow up. And because he is not slow to express this attitude, he is likely to be dismissed and marginalized by those fully in the adolescent fray. The precocious identifier is, to the others, a nerd, a wimp. His intellect and attainments may be considerable, but he is likely to be lonely and depressed when out of the company of adults who validate him. Precocious identifiers are likely to win scholastic and later preferments.

Professionally, they may advance dramatically and early, but they are very likely to face a distinctive crisis of their own when in early adulthood or midlife they find themselves consciously confronting the very same questions of identity and self-worth they were unable to experience in their teens.

But of course the great majority of adolescents are neither regressives nor precocious adults. They are, rather, held in a dynamic disequilibrium so dramatic, so periodically overwhelming, that responses which at any other time of life could fairly be labeled pathological are considered normative. James Dean, introducing his unforgettable teenage rebel without a cause in the film by that name, cries out in desperation: "You're tearing me apart!" He is addressing his parents, who are hopelessly blind to their son's predicament, cannot see it, cannot feel it, cannot help. For adolescents, the whole adult complex, including parents and teachers, is a kind of flimsily united call to join them, to be like them. But the adults who overtly or tacitly extend this invitation fail to see how inherently unappealing that invitation is.

The call to progress in a disciplined, orderly way to adulthood implies preparing for adult work. But terribly mixed, even forbidding messages are conveyed about adult work in the "real world." Adolescents are forcefully reminded that satisfying, remunerative, and exalted positions are few, the prospects of getting one more remote every year. One in a million, seemingly, becomes a trailblazing CEO or prominent professional or national political figure. The odds are discouragingly worse at succeeding in a field closer to an adolescent's heart: entertainment or big-time sports. What's more, the deferred rewards of any kind of work—and they are deferred indeed—are made out to be all but unattainable. Selective colleges are revealed to be more selective than ever, which says to the adolescent that not only is his future success dubious, but what looks to be the best next step to achieving it is chancy to impossible. Moreover, the adults extending the invitation to join them are not always, or even often, good advertisements for the adult condition. Even if they manage in their maturity to maintain some semblance of attractiveness and vitality, how many of them reveal genuine fulfillment and pleasure in their work and in their social roles? What do work, marriage, and parenting really look like from an adolescent's perspective? Does a boy see his father's satisfaction or ecstatic release in his job, in his family responsibilities, or is he more likely to sense those things when his father is home free, footloose, temporarily liberated by time off, a vacation, a few drinks?

To adolescents poised between the sweetly charged spirituality of childhood and the beckoning adult order, the best way ahead is very often to hang tight, to stay just where they are. Whereas the civic culture wants to see adolescence as a tender, challenging, difficult *stage*, the adolescent himself is more than willing to see it as a world unto itself, a world without end. "When I'm thirty," the hippie impresario Jerry Rubin wrote in *Do it!,* his 1970 counterculture manifesto, "my goal is to act like I'm fifteen." To adolescents everywhere, but especially to those densely packed into junior high schools, high schools, and colleges, the utopian dream of sheer peerhood, sheer brotherhood and sisterhood without hierarchy, adult judgment, or any crushing imperative to defer gratification and to work is often irresistible. For a time an adolescent feels himself living and even thriving in a highly developed subculture of *only* adolescence. Codes of behavior, speech, dress, and musical preferences are readable only by the initiates, the adolescents themselves. To attending adults they appear to be hypersensitive to any perceived threat to their autonomy and individuality, but they in fact have surrendered autonomy to the culture of their condition. In Erik Erikson's phrase, they have fallen under the sway of "cliques and crowds." In cliques they are able to alienate individual consciousness altogether into a kind of group will—and thus at times behave in what looks to adults to be a monstrously primitive or feral manner. Society is regularly shocked by their lapses and crimes. In crowds, in the migratory movements of youth and suspended youth who follow cultic rock bands like Phish or the Grateful Dead, there can be experienced an all-being surrender to Permanent Adolescence, to a world of Only Us, a Woodstock "nation," a world of Just This. Drugs that stimulate the mythy images and urges of the limbic brain, while slowing or bypassing altogether the brain's "higher," regulatory functions, are sometimes thought to be "the problem," but the better historical argument is that they are mere accelerators and enablers.

There is an optimistic (or is it desperate?) civic and therapeutic view of adolescence as a "stage," a developmental resting place before the adolescent moves on to the inevitable roles and responsibilities of functional young adulthood. This is a socially necessary view, and it is comforting, if true.

But the adolescent himself does not feel he is held in a "stage." Unaware consciously of how he arrived in such a condition, longing for the lilt and power of the puer world but unable to reenter, he is for a time spiritually stalled. This is Knight Percival, still and pensive on his mount, brooding over a stain of goose blood in the snow, no longer able to see the point of the quest. This is Holden Caulfield, a truant careering through the hollow sophistries of grownup Manhattan, on a doomed mission to regain the wholeness of his childhood. Such youth are in no position to accept the adult invitation, however warmly and sincerely offered. For it is practical adult reality that suppressed and disallowed the puer spirit in the first place, banishing it to memory, myth, and dream. The adolescent cannot save the puer, but he can offer mortal resistance to the adult order he sees rising so relentlessly on the near horizon.

Outwardly this resistance may look like rebellion, a youthful "counterculture." It can be active and provocative like the "flaming youth" of the American twenties or passive and detached like the aesthete dandies of Great Britain after World War I. Like the nineteenth century German youth who took to the forests and mountain paths in search of mystical union with the Transcendent, or their Parisian counterparts who assumed the world-denying attitudes of urban bohemianism, each succeeding generation of resistance is at heart the same. The Lost Generation, beats, hippies, generation X—names, postures, clothes may change, but all give form and expression to the adolescent refusal.

Assigning particular historical causes to the refusal may relieve some cultural anxiety, but such analysis carries little explanatory power. Trying to understand adolescent resistance in terms of cultural or demographic factors misses the more basic fact that the resistance is essentially individual and personal. Even overt political protest is a means to express the adolescent's personal resistance. However generalized the rhetoric, the drama is as personal and distinctive as each mother and daughter, father and son. Trying to read this drama as social history always distorts historical understanding. For, in fact, most youth of the American twenties were not jazz age cut-ups. A great majority of the sixties and seventies baby boom youth were not hippies or countercultural types. Indeed, in 1968, the first year American eighteen-year-olds could vote, a heavy majority voted for the Republican candidate for President, Richard Nixon.

Again, the recurring crisis of cultural generativity is played out between sons and fathers, daughters and mothers. It is also experienced between children and the first delegates called to stand in for parents: teachers, coaches, and counselors. The combined agents of the adult establishment insist that youth must learn and do culturally necessary things. Spiritually, the adolescent is aware that he has lost something prior and profound; to lose any more feels like spiritual death. No further cultural imperatives must threaten the adolescent's wildly improbable yet universal hope that he might still ascend, that he might reach a world both prior to and beyond the deadening "real world" he is being enjoined to serve: that he might get, not just high, but achieve the condition about which being high is an elusive hint.

Some of the gestures of adolescent resistance have clear social utility and thus recur with great regularity through the ages. Some sons defeat their fathers by exceeding them in accomplishment. Some confound their fathers by taking divergent, father-negating vocational paths. Hardheaded men of commerce are negated by artist or missionary or vagabond sons. The aging hippie beholds his accountant son with puzzlement. This kind of rebellion advances the social order and accounts for much essential work. But the son whose rebellion manifests itself in social productivity is fated to become an especially daunting father, one whose sons will be unable to see the redemptive, soul-saving nature of their father's rebellion, only the forbidding weight of its expectations. Those sons will experience the generational crisis in its fullest complexity and weight. They, like Hamlet and Holden Caulfield and every modern antihero, will question the point of living, of growing up at all—and they will mean it.

Adolescents do ask, in one way or another, whether there is any ultimate reason to forfeit the deep spiritual connectedness of childhood to the colder, emptier requirements of adulthood. My students ask, and some of them ask urgently. The very spirited ones struggle. Some rebel, defiantly make trouble. Some run away. Some withdraw and quit. A few take their lives.

But more than these despair. There is despair—the same despair—in those who, seemingly cowed and dutiful, go through the required motions. They are halting and inarticulate when asked about their condition. They do not sound convincing when they report: yeah, fine, everything's cool, no problem, whatever. We tell ourselves that this muting, this withdrawal is, after all, a *stage*. We take heart that they are, after all, delivering some or most of the expected goods. They are progressing; that is, freshmen become sophomores, sophomores become juniors. There is, after all, considerable compliance.

In this compliance no one wants to see the forging of a lifelong imposture.

# 2

## THE FIGURE OF ICARUS

IT IS NOT easy—in words, discursively—to account for the way a myth makes us understand. Myths are, of course, stories, and like any story they invite us to consider characters and predicaments. To read or hear or engage visually in the progression of a myth is to enter into it, to identify oneself with the god or hero and his or her circumstances. We also identify, not always consciously, with the teller, the intelligence shaping the story. Myths are unlike stories of "real life," whether naturalistic fiction or documentary accounts of assignable persons in assignable situations, in that we are aware—even as we pass wholeheartedly into our identifications—that god and hero do not exist in "real" historical time: that the rape of Leda by a divine swan or the metamorphosis of Daphne into a laurel tree did not occur in any possible time or place. Nor, like their close cousins, the parable and fable, are myths structured to engage us in moral lessons; that is, to convey practical truths, such as "slow and steady wins the race," through fanciful means: an anthropomorphic tortoise and hare.

Here, precisely, is the difficulty. When we enter a myth, we feel ourselves strangely and sometimes wonderfully changed, but there is no moral or lesson we can readily understand. A white bull from the sea seduces the Queen of Crete, and she gives birth to a monstrous

Minotaur. We are not usefully informed or improved by this story, but we are interested. We never quite understand it, but it and all of its stunning ramifications will not leave us alone.

The unease, the restlessness instilled by myths has motivated inspired minds to "decode" them, to reduce their capriciousness and irrationality to an orderly system from which practical and therapeutic conclusions can be drawn. Thus myths can be "interpreted," as Freud interpreted dreams and the Oedipus legend and as Bruno Bettelheim interpreted Grimm fairy tales, as symbolic representations of deep psychic wishes, wishes perhaps too disturbing, too destructive of civic order to be expressed directly. Bringing to conscious light this volatile material formerly repressed in unconscious recesses of the mind is the mission of Freudian psychoanalysis and, in a less scientific and more expansive key, the archetypal psychology of Carl Jung.

In Jungian terms, myths are "archetypal" phenomena. The stories are held to be universal structures, which, once engaged by the individual psyche, shape and energize it. The product of the engagement is only incidentally intellectual, if intellectual at all. The archetypes are working on us before we are working on them. One experiences myths—the archetypes—spiritually, with the full force of one's feeling. It is this kind of engagement, not intellectual explanation, that constitutes *knowing.* To know the intentions and full meaning of a myth requires that one simply enter into it. This has apparently been the method of scholar and writer Roberto Calasso in his compelling and wayward book, *The Marriage of Cadmus and Harmony*, a meditation on the meaning of myths through rapt retelling. Certain Jungians, too, as different in style and temperament as James Hillman and Robert Johnson, *begin* their explorations of archetypal material with strong tellings of the stories: the birth of Aphrodite, the quest of Percival, the romance of Tristan and Isolde. Johnson and Hillman ask good, fresh questions of these old stories and in many instances demonstrate the astonishing and troubling ways archetypal material illuminates contemporary human predicaments— illuminates but by no means fixes or solves.

THE FIGURE OF ICARUS    25

In the prologue to this book I proposed that the civic ideal upon which modern civilization rests may require an ultimately unsatisfying and unlivable imposture on the part of the youth called upon to maintain that order. There is an enduring myth that illuminates this problem. It is the story of Daedalus and Icarus. The fullest and most familiar version of the story is recounted in the Roman poet Ovid's *Metamorphoses*, a compendium in verse of the myths of classical antiquity, composed in the first years of the Christian era. Daedalus and Icarus are also referred to by other classical and medieval writers, including Apollodorus, Plutarch, Scholiast, Hyginus, Pliny, Fulgentius, Diodorus Siculus, Pausanias, Servius, Virgil, Suidas, Photius, Isadore of Seville, Zenobius, Plato, and Herodotus. Wherever Western culture has since taken root, the myth has been translated and told. The story of Daedalus and Icarus has also been a recurring subject of sculpture and painting in the West.

Here is the story:

*Daedalus, the renowned Athenian craftsman and smith, was stranded in exile on the island of Crete with his young son, Icarus. The Cretan King, Minos, originally invited Daedalus to the island for the purpose of designing a great maze to contain the Minotaur, a monstrous being with a man's body and a bull's head. The Minotaur was the illicit product of the unnatural union of Minos's queen, Pasiphae, and a white bull who emerged mysteriously from the sea. (The bull was in fact sent by the god Poseidon, who had long lusted after Pasiphae.)*

*The maze containing the Minotaur was so ingeniously devised that, once led inside, no mortal, save the architect himself, could escape its confines. But when Minos grew suspicious that Daedalus had divulged the secret of escape, the king forbade his guest to leave the kingdom, specifying that he must not depart the island by sea.*

*Longing to regain his freedom and to escape the troubled kingdom, Daedalus, ever the inventive engineer, sat about devising a way to escape the* island—but not by the sea. His earlier researches had revealed the utility of animal parts in achieving desirable human outcomes. A brilliant nephew, Perdix, had once demonstrated how a tool modeled on a fish jaw could serve as an excellent saw. So, drawing on his knowledge of the way gradations of reeds were fitted together to make musical pipes and studying closely the structure of birds' wings, he began the construction of two substantial sets of wings, one for himself and one for Icarus.

The construction of the wings was a laborious and deliberate process. If the wings were to bear the father's and son's weight aloft in the powerful winds coursing over the Aegean, they would have to be well crafted and durable. Daedalus gathered together eagle feathers and sewed the larger ones together with flaxen thread. The smaller feathers were held in place by wax gathered from bees.

The work of constructing these sets of wings demanded all of Daedalus's concentration and skill. He attempted to explain to his son what he was doing, but Icarus was not interested. He was charmed by the idea of actually flying like a bird, free and unrestrained, but he had no time for the tedious, exacting process of construction. So as Daedalus toiled on, Icarus laughed and played and sought ways to amuse himself.

At last the wings were finished, and Daedalus saw that they were good. The important thing now was for Daedalus to get Icarus's attention and to explain to him how to fly safely. It was essential that the boy stay close to his father. In addition, there were two essential principles to be observed. First, Icarus was told to take care to fly high enough above the waves that the wings would not be struck and damaged. Even more crucially, he was not to fly too high, too close to the sun, because the heat would melt the wax, and the wings would come apart. "You must fly the middle course," Icarus was told.

All of this Daedalus explained carefully, but Icarus, who was impatient to be aloft in his new wings, may not have taken it in.

Daedalus launched his son into the air and then arose himself. At first all was well as father and son gained altitude and headed northeast over the Aegean. Those below on the island looked up to see something amazing: two winged figures, a boy and a man, flying!

Icarus was enchanted, thrilled to be riding the wind, high above the spar-

*kling sea. It felt so good, so exhilarating, this feeling of flight, that he wanted to fly even higher, to ascend to the very height of heaven. And so up and up he went—to his father's horror. For he had forgotten Daedalus's warning, his careful instructions to keep to the "middle course." Just as Daedalus had feared, the hot rays of sunlight melted the wax holding Icarus's wings intact. Soon Icarus was falling, falling fast.*

*Daedalus scanned the surface of the sea looking for Icarus but saw only a scattering of feathers floating in the brine. Icarus was drowned, and only later would Daedalus discover his lifeless body and carry it to the shore of an island, which now bears his name. The weeping Daedalus buried his son, and as he kissed his cheek, Daedalus had a sense that these would be the last kisses he would ever give.*

This account, more or less as Ovid tells it in the *Metamorphoses*, has a familiar feeling to it, a kind of resonance—even at first reading or hearing. Like archetypal material generally, the story is interesting but curiously unsurprising. We seem to know in advance that Icarus will not heed his father's warnings, that the instruction and training will not take. Icarus, as briefly sketched, is pure puer, carefree in his play as his father executes a considered plan. It is clearly Icarus's fault that he plummets and perishes. He has not listened. He has flown too high. As a cautionary tale, the story warns against youthful impetuosity. But the myth is strangely lacking in power as a cautioning tale. Icarus's headstrong daring is actually more thrilling than dreadful. We tend not to ponder whether Icarus was careless or defiant; we are fascinated, rather, by the fatal inevitability of his ascent.

The essential truth about Icarus is not that he is headstrong or reckless or disobedient. The essential truth is that he is a boy. As it happens, Ovid addresses the moral implications of headstrong youth in another myth of flight, the story of Phaethon and the sun god Apollo.

*Young Phaethon, born of the Sun god, Phoebus Apollo, and the mortal Clymene, was infuriated one day when the youthful Epaphus challenged his claim that he* was in fact the child of the sun. Phaethon went at once to Clymene and told her of the insult. Clymene was incensed and swore a mortal oath that Phaethon was indeed sired by the divine Phoebus. She then dispatched the boy to Apollo's court so that he might be reassured by the god himself.

So Phaethon departed immediately on the eastward journey to the royal palace of the sun. There Phoebus greeted the boy and affirmed at once his paternity. So ardent was Apollo in his protestations that he vowed he would grant Phaethon anything he asked as proof of his fatherly devotion.

Phaethon was quick to respond. He told Apollo he wanted to drive the royal chariot of the sun and its fiery steeds through a full day's journey over the earth.

The instant he heard the request, Apollo was overcome with foreboding and remorse. He tried with all his force and wit to dissuade Phaethon, stressing the strength and skill necessary to hold the wildly spirited horses in their traces. Once off the celestial tracks, the chariot and its life-giving radiance would plummet disastrously to earth, scorching it to devastation. The daily course of the solar chariot, Phoebus pleaded, was not a picturesque tour over majestic cities; it was a breakneck gallop past every danger and calamity. In truth Apollo could not imagine Phaethon, or any youth, managing the feat.

But Phaethon would not yield, so Apollo, who had made his promise to the boy on pain of death itself, attempted with a heavy heart to teach his son how to drive the sun through the day. Applying a magic salve to Phaethon's face to shield him from the terrible heat, Apollo urged him to be moderate. He was admonished to spare the whip and rein in the chargers at all costs.

> Keep to this route; my wheel tracks there show plain.
> Press not too low nor strain your course too high;
> too high, you'll burn heaven's palaces;
> too low, the earth; the safest course lies in between.[1]

Like Daedalus cautioning his Icarus, Apollo told Phaethon to stick to the middle course, avoiding extremes.

Phaethon was too transported with anticipation to listen. Rapt with joy, he mounted the gold and bejeweled car and seized the reins. Phaethon could only shout thanks to his remorseful father before the gates restraining the steeds were lifted and the chariot lurched into its fateful flight.

Bearing so light and light-handed a load, the chariot pitched and bounced wildly and was soon off the celestial tracks, careering from side to side in steep, unguided descent. Unable to hold the reins and feeling the unbearable radiance through the soles of his feet, Phaeton's fear arose sickeningly. Now he bewailed his terrible wish and longed to be earthbound; how happily he would forfeit his claim to divine parentage.

But it was too late. The white-hot chariot hurtled earthward out of control. The startled moon noted with wonder her brother's downward trajectory as the chariot passed below her. Then the clouds themselves were scalded, and mountain peaks erupted in flame. Great cities burned to ash, crops were seared white, and the green earth was parched to brown cracks. The very rivers ignited or were scalded dry, and featureless islands arose suddenly as the seas receded. The seething chariot baked the skins of Africans black and left a vast Sahara of ashen dust.

Patient Mother Earth herself rose up finally to complain to God:

> If fire destroys me, let the fire be thine:
> My doom were lighter felt by thy design! . . .
> See my singed hair! Ash in my eyes, ash on my lips so deep!
> Are these the fruits of my fertility?
> Is this for duty done the due return?[2]

Mother Earth spoke truly. Creation itself was in peril. Jove, the father almighty, ascended the very height of heaven where he exclaimed in thunder and dispatched a bolt, which struck Phaethon from the chariot and killed him.

Fires fought to extinguish fires over the devastated earth. Phaethon, his auburn locks in flame, glided through the night sky like a shooting star. His body came to rest half a world away in a distant sea. Nymphs recovered his remains and buried them in a tomb by a river bank. Someone carved an epigraph in stone.

> HERE PHAETHON LIES, HIS FATHER'S CHARIOTEER—
> GREAT WAS HIS FALL, YET GREATLY DID HE DARE.[3]

Phaethon and Icarus are superficially parallel figures. Both attempt a flight they will prove unable to complete. Both are oblivious to their fathers' practical counsel. Both perish. But in very revealing ways, they are dissimilar. Phaethon is demanding and imperious. An insult to his pride motivates him to seek out his father and insist on, literally, taking the adult reins. Phaethon attempts what he is inherently unable to do; he assumes the role of a father he has not yet become. Icarus, by contrast, harbors no such desires, makes no such demands. He expresses no wish to be Daedalus. His interest in flight is not to prove himself or to be powerful. He seeks only sensation and ecstasy. Whereas Phaethon attempted to do the world's most generative and essential work, Icarus wanted only to play.

Considered this way, Phaethon's story is a myth of adolescence, Icarus's a myth of boyhood. Phaethon, shamed by the taunt of a peer, assumes his father's role—a disastrous imposture. His flight is doomed from the very outset. As soon as the chariot's team is released, Phaethon is in trouble:

> But lightly weights the yoke; the chariot moves
> With ease unwanted, suspect buoyancy;
> And like a ship at sea unballasted
> That pitches in the sea for lack of weight,
> The chariot now, lacking its usual load,
> Bounced driverless in empty leaps.[4]

Icarus, by contrast, flies surely and well on his brand new wings, wings designed just for him. It is not any ineptitude on his part that is fatal, but his joy. Unlike Phaethon, he expresses no wish to be a god, but in Ovid's account he is thought to be godlike by those observing from land. With his father, high above the islands and sparkling sea, "the boy began to enjoy his thrilling flight and left his guide to roam the ranges of the heaven."[5]

Phaethon goes down in terror; Icarus ascends—thrillingly self-assured—to the light.

As suggested already, Icarus is a true puer. As such he cannot be otherwise, cannot be improved. Yet his father, who knows something of the world, strives earnestly to bend him, to educate him to the world's ways, if only that he might live. The myth dramatizes the archetypal—and seemingly unresolvable—tension between son and father. But perhaps it is misleading to call it a tension "between" father and son, for the tension is all Daedalus's. The myth is a moral lesson only from the Daedalus/adult perspective. Only from that perspective, too, is the myth tragic—tragic in that Icarus's loss is inevitable and unpreventable. From that perspective the myth's teller seems to look directly into our eyes and shrug: that is how it is with fathers, and that is how it is with sons. An accomplished father like Daedalus knows how things work practically and how to make one's way viably through the world. A son like Icarus cannot know such things; he knows only the allure of dreams and dreamy play.

As it happens, there is more to the myth than this straightforward generational dilemma. Indeed, the result might have been otherwise.

To understand the deeper implications of the myth requires a consideration of Daedalus's experience prior to his exile on Crete. When he was still a welcome and much celebrated guest on the island, Daedalus was contracted by King Minos to design a maze that would contain the dreaded Minotaur. The maze would be no mere prison for a public menace. It would shield from any public viewing the secret of the queen's bestial infidelity. Daedalus's engineering feat served to cover up the stunning evidence of a shameful royal error the civic order did not want to acknowledge.

In the accounts of the ancient writers Diodorus Siculus and Apollodorus, Daedalus was even more deviously implicated in the crime, as he is said to have devised the means by which Pasiphae had intercourse with the bull: by inserting herself inside a cowlike structure designed by Daedalus.

As it happened, Daedalus was at the time no stranger to crime and deception. Back in his native Athens, he committed a repellent blood crime: the murder of his precociously talented nephew, Perdix.

Perdix was only twelve when his mother gave him over to her brother Daedalus's care and guidance. Lucky as he was in being apprenticed to such a brilliant engineer, Perdix's own technical accomplishments were starting to win him public acclaim. It was said that Perdix made a study of a fish spine and was able to replicate it exactly. Moreover, using a jawbone of serrated fish teeth as a template, he invented the saw. He also fastened two metal arms at a hinged point to produce the first mechanical compass.

These inspired accomplishments of his talented ward made Daedalus murderously jealous. On a pretense of research, Daedalus led his nephew up to the pinnacle of Athena's temple at the height of the acropolis—and threw him headlong to his death. In some accounts the spirit of the falling boy is transformed into a partridge by Athena, who is a patroness of talent.

The crime did not go unnoticed. When Daedalus attempted to stuff the broken, lifeless body of Perdix into a canvas bag, some passers-by were suspicious of bloodstains on the sack and challenged Daedalus. Daedalus claimed he had bagged a dead serpent and was hauling it away in keeping with Athenian statutes. But suspicions mounted, and when formal charges were brought against Daedalus, he fled to Crete.

There, both before and briefly after the completion of the maze, he enjoyed the status of a celebrated guest, until he fell out of favor with the king. His talent had always resided in seeing the familiar from a novel perspective: thinking, to use a contemporary term, "out of the box." So, since Minos had expressly ordered him not to depart the island by water, and since the formidable Cretan navy was to be on guard against any such escape, Daedalus sought to find a way to depart by air, though no mortal had been able to do this yet.

Daedalus chose the simplest, most obvious approach to the problem of human flight. Birds fly; the means are wings. Therefore he would construct wings. The genius here is not in the conception but in the execution. The fabrication must be excellent; the wings must work. Ovid is precise in his account of their construction.

> *Row upon row of feathers he arranged;*
> *The smallest first, then larger ones, to form*
> *A growing graded shape, as rustic pipes*
> *Rise in a gradual slope of lengthening reeds;*
> *Then bound the middle and the base with wax*
> *And flaxen threads, and bent them, so arranged,*
> *Into a gentle curve to imitate*
> *Wings of a real bird.*[6]

All of this precision is lost on the puer.

> *Young Icarus, who blithely unaware*
> *He plays with his own peril, tries to catch*
> *Feathers that float upon the wandering breeze,*
> *Or softens with his thumb the yellow wax,*
> *And by his laughing mischief interrupts*
> *His father's wondrous work.*[7]

Of course the master builder's ingenuity would not have been lost on his nephew Perdix. Perdix's shrewd observation of the fish jaw as prototype for the saw could well have been the inspiration for Daedalus's wings project. Perdix would have been most attentive and helpful. He would have appreciated the wings' capacity and also their limitations. He would have watched, listened, understood. He would know better than to fly too close to the sun.

Daedalus is utterly ineffective in holding Icarus's attention; his tuition goes completely unheeded. In this failure lies the sense of inevitability pervading the myth. The puer spirit is not only impervious to adult industry and practical instruction, he *laughs* at it. In the face of this imperviousness, Daedalus is helpless. The wings work, but he loses his son. There is no generativity.

There is no generativity on two counts. Icarus does not carry on his father's work because he prefers the heights of heaven to prudence and mere viability. Perdix, a natural apprentice, does not carry on Daedalus's work because he is murdered in jealousy. For, at heart, Daedalus is less in love with the wonder of material transformation—his art—than he is in love with the power and status his gifts have won him. His masterpiece, the maze, served to conceal the royal shame of Crete. There is no lasting satisfaction for him in this; he longs to be free of this weight, to escape. But there is every suggestion in the myth that there can be no escape for one who has so ruthlessly extinguished real genius, real talent. Daedalus was an architect, a smith, an engineer. In killing Perdix he could not have imagined that he was killing genius and talent itself. So what exactly did he think he was killing? He wanted to kill a boy. He wanted to kill the *spirit* of the boy who had been so marvelously endowed. Perhaps he believed he could hoard that kind of spirit, keep it to himself, as if it were some kind of amassable quantity. Perhaps he feared he was losing it or might lose it and thus found its bright presence in his nephew unendurable.

In these myths both "heirs" perish, while Daedalus continues to make his problematic way in the world. Later he will surface in Sicily and conspire with the royal family to murder King Minos, who has come there to find him.

Daedalus is deeply saddened by the death of Icarus, but he is not wiser for the loss. The renowned builder and father who had patiently counseled "the middle course" for his spirited son is not finally a shining example of the virtues that result from adhering to such a course. His position in the world can be seen as a kind of "middle course," from which his son was quick to ascend and from which his nephew was hurled brutally down to earth. Daedalus, whatever his guilt and grief, is a survivor. He is much valued, as he was in Sicily, for fabricating "delightful toys" for royalty. But there is also something hollow, failed, forever unrealized in him. This is suggested in the myth when, as Daedalus is bestowing his last tearful kisses on the face of his dead son, he is suddenly distracted.

*A chattering, partridge in a muddy ditch watched him*
*And clapped its wings and crowed for joy.*[8]

This is Perdix, transformed into a bird. The ancients were the first to note that the partridge (*Perdix perdix*) nests on the ground or in the lower branches of hedges. Though fully winged, it was believed to be wary of taking flight. The name Perdix derives from the Latin verb *perdere,* which means "to lose." The nominal form, perdix, means ruined, done-for, hopeless, lost.

# 3

# THE EXILE OF DAEDALUS AND THE DAWN OF MODERN CONSCIOUSNESS

DAEDALUS REPRESENTS A striking departure from the figures who surround him in classical mythology. His genius neither derives from nor is it expressed in deep forces of nature. Unlike the gods and heroes, he is more deliberate than he is spontaneous or spirited. His gift is applied science: combining materials to achieve practical ends. He is not an artist; he does not aim to move the heart or to inspire. He is an engineer; his aims are utilitarian, instrumental. He is concerned with means, not ends, and thus his value in the mythological order is his service to those in power.

Moreover, as we have seen, Daedalus is a criminal. He jealously murders his nephew Perdix, and he first deceives and later plots to assassinate his former patron, Minos. It might be said that, while impressive and in a superficial way delightful to his royal employers, Daedalus's works are less than wondrous. His most famous achievement, the Cretan maze, succeeds in caging the Minotaur and imprisoning whatever mortal unfortunates are sentenced to its confines, but this is not an elevating achievement. As established already, the maze is contracted by Minos to contain a monster—and to conceal the shame of his queen's bestial lust. The wings Daedalus fashions for Icarus and himself are only a partial success—good, perhaps, but not good enough. Later in Sicily his imaginative toys are a delight to the young women of the royal household. His last known achievement is to construct a system of piping that enables him to scald visiting King Minos to death in his bath.

Daedalus's work is reactive. With the exception of the wings, his inventions are occasioned by the desires of others. Moreover, no classical account of Daedalus suggests that he takes any positive pleasure in his achievements. He arrives in Crete a criminal exile. He colludes with the queen to gratify her lust for Poseidon's bull. In the sordid aftermath, he builds the maze. Out of favor with the King and under a kind of house arrest, he conceives of the wings project, which results in the death of his only son.

Neither a hero nor a satisfyingly tragic figure, Daedalus is nonetheless civilization's prototypical engineer. As such, he represents a transition in Western mythology from a sensibility of pure, unfettered desire to one of practical scheming. Daedalus presents the first clear challenge and alternative to classical mythology's theology of desire. Until Daedalus, mythological metamorphoses were both magical and "natural," in the sense that a natural element in creation, like a nymph or a youth, might be transformed into another natural element, such as a tree or a constellation. Were the gods at work, it is easy to imagine them transforming Pasiphae into a cow for the purposes of mating with Poseidon's bull. As noted earlier, when the goddess Athena feared Perdix was plummeting to an unjust demise, she quickly embodied his descending spirit as a partridge. Daedalus is incapable of such magic, but he attempts a limited, material imitation: he makes his son not a bird, but birdlike, with fabricated wings. The wings work—to a "middle course" extent—without aid of magic, without aid of the gods. Those first working wings constructed just as Ovid describes might well work today. They are a true prototype of modern aviation, and modern aviation is an excellent emblem of a world in which applied technology is believed to reveal ultimate reality. In that world, in that monument to Daedalus, the gods and spirit of classical antiquity are banished to the seemingly harmless preserves of fancy, art, and dreams. And thus has Western civilization progressed from capricious metaphysics—superstition—to empirical, perpetually self-correcting science. Yet, it must be remembered, this was no triumph for Daedalus. Daedalus wept inconsolably as he buried his drowned son. It was on the cheek of the dead and dreamy Icarus that Daedalus offered his last kisses. The wings had worked, but something essential was lost.

Daedalus seems never to have been happy or fulfilled while in exile on Crete. Carrying the weight of his bloodguilt for having murdered his twelve-year-old nephew, he knew also that the boy's grief-stricken mother, his sister, had taken her life. Colluding with Pasiphae to construct the device by which she could have intercourse with the white bull brought only trouble in the aftermath, as did the construction of the maze. He was perhaps sustained by the birth of a son, Icarus, whose mother was a slave in Minos's household. But Daedalus was clearly a *persona non grata* when he conceived his plan of escape.

In Ovid's account, Icarus is untroubled by his father's burdens. The boy is irrepressibly playful and cheerful. His innocence and his imperviousness to the practical business before Daedalus suggest that he is of an altogether different—prior?—order of being from his father. Just as his father is held to task by desperate, practical necessity, Icarus is held in the thrall of pleasure and of play. Fully aware of this—the boy cavorts and teases openly as his father toils—Daedalus does nothing to correct him. If Daedalus represents the advent of the Practical Scheme in Western mythology, his son and heir will have none of it. The ethereal Icarus will soon be literally so. What, one wonders, is his special significance to Daedalus, who has shown himself to be anything but patiently paternal to his nephew? Daedalus appears to be resigned to, even respectful of, the boy's flamboyant inattention. What might

Icarus sense or know that has granted him such autonomy before the great engineer?

Icarus is *puer eternis*. He embodies the spirit of limitless play. Given the chance, he would ascend to the height of heaven. Ecstatic communion is his nature. Daedalus has lost that nature, and he has killed Perdix, a promising boy, a boy whose gifts and inclinations were like his own. Moreover, he killed Perdix when he was twelve years old—poised at the brink of adult responsibility. Daedalus's gifts were discoverable; they could be taught, learned, replicated. Indeed a mere twelve-year-old had shown himself proficient in his uncle's trade. Daedalus's applied science reduced whole, vital beings—eagles—to mere mechanical function: working wings. By murdering Perdix, Daedalus reduces him to a flightless bird.

Stricken by Daedalus, Perdix will not fly again. But Icarus would fly. Icarus would forget or refuse to learn his wings' limitations. Icarus flies in the face of the very idea of limitation. In providing his son the opportunity to ascend, Daedalus released a spirit greater than he knew. Daedalus was unaware that there was more to his wings than mere mechanical function.

In assembling the wings out of feathers, wax, and flaxen thread, Daedalus has in mind the structure of an ancient instrument, the syrinx, or pipes of Pan.

> Row upon row of feathers he arranged,
> The smallest first, then larger ones, to form
> A growing graded shape, as rustic pipes
> Rise in a gradual slope of lengthening reeds.[1]

Pan's pipes were also a fabrication, and like the wings project, the pipes were a substitution for something vital and urgent—and forever lost.

According to her myth, Syrinx was a lovely water nymph, beloved of her naiad sisters and the other woodland sprites of Arcadia. She was so like Diana in beauty and bearing that she could be mistaken for the goddess—and once was. The goat-footed Pan spotted her as he returned from his mountain revels and set upon her to ravish her. Like her adored Diana, Syrinx had devoted herself to chastity, and as Pan bore down on her, she begged the watery naiads to change her form. Thus as Pan reached to embrace her, his arms closed over a cluster of marsh reeds. Their plaintive music as the wind passed through them touched Pan's heart, and he cut them to graded lengths and fixed them together with wax, so that the instrument and its music would stay with him forever.

In the story of Syrinx, a musical instrument is fashioned out of sheer desire. It is a substitute, a compensation. In the story of Daedalus, an instrument of flight is fashioned after these pipes of Pan. Considered this way, the wings—and the "middle course" of their intended use— are two removes from the elemental desire that drove the myths of classical antiquity into being. Daedalus's achievement is thus to complete a progression from desire to music to technology.

From a twenty-first century perspective—the perspective of the Age of Technology—Daedalus might be considered the herald of a new consciousness in the classical world: the consciousness of utility and mechanical transformation. In this new consciousness, the function of an eagle's wing is abstracted from the organic unity of the eagle. The function of a fish's spine or jaw is abstracted from the fish. The function, the principle is durable—perhaps immortal. The eagle and the fish are perishable; they are, seen in this way, mere occasions and opportunities for ingenious use.

From a contemporary perspective, then, Daedalus is an avatar of progress. But the new consciousness cannot express what it has lost. It is inherently numb to desire and deaf to music. It destroys its spirited heirs; and its schemes serve only to realize the crimes and passing desires of the regimes that embrace it.

From the standpoint of modernity, Icarus is foolish, fatally foolish. The puer spirit—desire itself—is fatally foolish. The only course is the "middle course." The urge to ascend, the impulse to ecstasy is to be suppressed and outgrown. In modern consciousness the puer spirit is not ultimately real; the passage of boys through the "middle course" to functional manhood is ultimately real. This reality is validated by functional utility, by the sustainability of persons and regimes over chronological time. What other reality, modern consciousness asks, could there be?

Daedalus, it has been proposed, distinguished himself among his mythological brethren by his knack for converting elements of nature to mechanical use. It has been proposed also that these accomplishments did not fulfill him, although they enabled him to survive. The elevation of Daedalus's knack for fabrication to a dominant worldview requires some explanation, since who—knowing his story—would wish to be Daedalus?

Within the mythological order itself, none of Daedalus's achievements was a triumph—or even much of a success. Something elemental would have to change in the consciousness of the classical world for the suspect fabrications of a figure like Daedalus to set a new standard for human purpose.

Introducing his school text, *Hellas,* a history of ancient Greece, Cyril Robinson contrasted the worldview of a fifth-century B.C.E. Athenian to that of a modern Westerner in the following way. Given a preference, Robinson wrote, between a stirring poem or a momentous breakthrough in bridge construction or medicine, the Athenian would take the poem every time. Such a choice bewilders modern man. What could have caused such a dramatic shift in worldview?

In his youthful masterpiece, *The Birth of Tragedy (Out of the Spirit of Music),* Friedrich Nietzsche charts a portentous transformation of western consciousness in the development of Attic tragedy in the fifth century B.C.E. Nietzsche argues that this shift in worldview came about because of the civic need to reconcile two titanic—and perhaps irreconcilable—human impulses: the primordial urge to express unrestrained desire and the enlightened drive to create beauty and order. Each of these forces is championed by an "art god" of the Greek pantheon. Nietzsche saw in Dionysus the expression of mankind's elemental desire. Dionysus's story is sensual, orgiastic, and ecstatic; it is dangerous if not downright destructive to civil order, and in its ultimate expression the individual's sense of identity, including social place and civic responsibility, is obliterated in ecstatic communion. The opposing tendency was expressed for Nietzsche by Apollo, the "shining one." Apollo represents light, clarity, harmony, beauty, and proportion. Apollonian truth is expressed in concrete images: in sculpture, architecture, and epic, narrative poetry. Dionysian truth is more elemental and thus pre-imagistic; its arts are music and dance—but not polite, decorative music and dance. Dionysian art is an ecstatic rite; it invites its celebrants to oblivion.

The Dionysian and Apollonian principles are seemingly irreconcilable, and Nietzsche saw them running historically parallel to one another, alternately or serially capturing mankind's allegiance, until they were by a "metaphysical miracle of the Hellenic will,"[2] conjoined in the Attic tragedies of Aeschylus and Sophocles.

The Apollonian and Dionysian tendencies, Nietzsche wrote, are realized in different modes of experience, the Apollonian in constructed "dreams," the Dionysian in "intoxication." By shaping and transforming lived existence into "beautiful illusion," Apollonian dreams help make conscious life "possible and worth living."[3]

Prior to any such aesthetic transformation of experience, the Dionysian impulse was at work in the world. Nietzsche located it in the rituals of intoxication and abandon celebrated in ancient Asia Minor and Babylon, migrating later to the Greek and Italian peninsulas, persisting into the European Middle Ages in the form of the St. John and St. Vitus dances. If the civic aim of the Apollonian dream is to hold up conscious images of a beautiful and worthy life, the aim of the Dionysian revel is to obliterate individual consciousness altogether and to reimmerse celebrants in the teeming, generative power of nature.

Under the charm of the Dionysian not only is the reunion between man and man reaffirmed, but nature which has become alienated, hostile, or subjugated, celebrates once more her reconciliation with her lost son, man. . . .

In song and in dance man expresses himself as a member of a higher community . . . he feels himself a god, he himself now walks about enchanted, in ecstasy. . . . He is no longer an artist, he has become a work of art: in these paroxysms of intoxication the artistic power of all nature reveals itself to the highest gratification of primordial unity.[4]

Nietzsche saw in the gradual emergence of the first Greek tragedies an artistic combining of the Dionysian and Apollonian tendencies. The genius of Aeschylus and Sophocles, as he saw it, was not to fuse the two great forces, but rather to hold both in an uneasy but charged equilibrium so that both Dionysian feeling and Apollonian appreciation could be experienced. Audiences of the early tragedies are moved in ways they cannot fully articulate. The experience is at once unreal—like a dream—but somehow ultrareal. The plays evoke terrible, terrifying feelings, also ecstatic ones. The cathartic moments in great theater feel, more than anything else, like intoxication.

Understood historically, Greek theater—the tragedies, satyr plays, and comedies—evolved out of primitive harvest festivals. At their heart was a deep impulse to worship, and the object of worship was Dionysus, his spirit and his story. At first, this impulse was expressed in orgiastic abandon in the course of ancient fertility rites. These had, by the dawning of Athenian theater, become ritualized into set dances that suggested some aspect of Dionysus's story. In time the dancing choruses began to chant and to declaim. Then a legendary character, Thespis, was said to have stepped out of the chorus and to have spoken— "acted"—as an individual. Soon there was a second "thespian," and then, in an innovation attributed to Sophocles himself, a third—and the art of Attic theater was born.

Even when institutionalized citywide as the annual Festival of Dionysus, the early Athenian theater looked back with reverence to the pre-civil spirit of the "wine-faced god." In time the enactments of Dionysian stories would give way to other mythic and tragic subject matter; but in two critical ways, the civic theater—the seeming reconciliation of Dionysian and Apollonian tendencies—never failed to acknowledge its older, wilder origins. The first of these acknowledgments was the performance of the satyr plays with their unapologetic celebration of bestial energy and lust. The second, as Nietzsche wrote, was the cathartic response to the tragedies on the part of the audiences. In their rapt engagement, audiences collectively shed practical, moral consciousness and lost themselves in the drama. This is, in effect, a sublimation of the earlier, more instinctual response of the original Dionysian orgiasts in which, Nietzsche speculated, individual consciousness once gave way to collective ecstatic oblivion. In the great tragedies the culturally dangerous and intolerable elements are experienced deeply, but, thanks to artistic transformation, only partially, which is to say psychologically:

> The horrible "witches' brew" of sensuality and cruelty becomes ineffective; only the curious blending and duality in the emotions of the Dionysian revelers remind us—as medicines remind us of deadly poison—of the phenomenon that pain begets joy, that ecstasy may wring sounds of agony from us. At the very climax of joy there sounds a cry of horror or a yearning lamentation for an irretrievable loss.[5]

Seen this way, tragic theater's dissolution of individual consciousness into collective catharsis allows the kind of release provided earlier by ecstatic dancing and by dithyrambic music—themselves subverbal expressions of the Dionysian impulse.

From the standpoint of civil, ethical modernity, the progression from orgiastic rite to tragic theater is a good example of progress. Nietzsche's disturbing suggestion is, while acknowledging the greatness of the

Hellenic achievement, that this progression is a compromise, and even a loss, of something elemental to a fully human life. Nietzsche protested that the validity of his claim could not possibly be seen unless the veils of contemporary timidity and piety were lifted. Here Nietzsche fires an early salvo in the direction of the Christian spirituality of his age:

> Whoever approaches those Olympians with another religion in his heart, searching among them for moral elevation, even for sanctity, for disincarnate spirituality, for charity and benevolence, will soon be forced to turn his back on them, discouraged and disappointed. For there is nothing [in Olympic figures such as Dionysus and Apollo] that suggests asceticism, spirituality, or duty.[6]

Such veils are not lifted easily. Christian religious practice can be seen as the very negation of, or antidote to, the Dionysian impulse— and to the Homeric pantheon generally. This for Nietzsche was the ultimate violation of given truth. Nietzsche saw in Christianity a deep "hostility to life,"[7] which gave rise to a relentless search for "another" life, "another" world. This "hatred" of the given world led Christians, Nietzsche wrote, to a "condemnation of the passions" and a "fear of beauty and sensuality." Harboring such fears, Christians cannot finally bear art or pleasure, and out of this forbearance conventional Christian morality was born. The most sacred act in such a scheme is to be crucified and transported to "another" world. By contrast, to the Homeric man, the given world was infused with divine delight.

> Existence under the bright sunshine of such gods is regarded as desirable in itself, and the real pain of Homeric men is caused by parting from it.[8]

Approaching the story of Icarus and Daedalus with "another religion"—that is non-Homeric religion—in one's heart can cause similar problems of interpretation. In the non- or post-Homeric view,

Icarus impetuously squanders his life in pursuit of an impossible thrill. But considered in the light of another theology, one in which, as Nietzsche writes, "existence under the bright sunshine of such gods is regarded as desirable in itself," Icarus is on a divine course. It is the more practical, more world-wary and world-weary Daedalus who wants to avoid premature combustion. To the Homeric sensibility it is Daedalus who parts from the higher reality—in favor of something altogether novel and imperfectly understood: a prudent "middle course."

For Nietzsche it is Apollo's ethical aspect—"know thyself," "nothing in excess"—that clouds the older, truer Dionysian impulse. The Apollonian tendency is to create a beautiful illusion—art—to check the darker impulses of Dionysian desire. In the interplay between the two, there is no creative "synthesis," no tempering or softening. Rather, the Apollonian and Dionysian tendencies simply alternate in an uneasy relationship.

> And so, wherever the Dionysian prevailed, the Apollonian was checked and destroyed. But, on the other hand, it is equally certain that wherever the Dionysian onslaught was successfully withstood, the authority and majesty of the Delphic god exhibited itself more rigid and menacing than ever.[9]

For Nietzsche, then, the Dionysian is born of nature, the Apollonian of culture. Moreover, Nietzsche contends, nature is true, culture a lie.[10]

According to this conviction, the true archetype of man is the Dionysian satyr:

> . . . the archetype of man, the embodiment of his highest and most intense emotions, the ecstatic reveler . . . one who proclaims wisdom from the very heart of nature, a symbol of the sexual omnipotence of nature which the Greeks used to contemplate with reverent wonder.[11]

In contrast to the erotically charged Greeks, modern man, Nietzsche contended, "timorously and mawkishly" prefers to see natural man as "a sentimental, flute-playing tender shepherd." The gentle shepherd is a sentimental negation of the satyr, and Christ, the ideal type of such shepherds—both shepherd and lamb—serves only to emasculate and dispirit the truer, prior satyr-man.

The Apollonian, civilizing tendency wants to banish the untamed nature of Dionysus by, literally, *enlightening* it: illuminating the darkness. Wisdom, even more surely than civility and moderation, will still the natural/Dionysian man's urges to excess and oblivion. For Nietzsche, wisdom is "a crime against nature." Nietzsche believed the greatest tragedians, Sophocles and Aeschylus, knew this and embedded this terrifying truth in their plays. Nietzsche maintains that the wisdom of Oedipus—his riddle-solving, truth-discovering capacity—is the horrific consequence of *violating* nature. Thus Oedipus is graced with the wisdom to solve the riddle of the sphinx *because* he has monstrously violated his nature by murdering his father and desiring his mother. In the same manner and for the same reasons is civil justice enthroned at the conclusion of *The Oresteia:* because of the child sacrifice, parricide, and other unnatural longings of the house of Atreus. When those cross-generational blood crimes come fully to light, wisdom and civil justice rise to ascendancy—but at the cost of mankind's true nature, of his authentic life.

Nietzsche charts this loss of primal authenticity in the gradual removal of the Dionysian tendency in Greek tragic art. And if Dionysian expression is the very wellspring of tragedy, and of human vitality itself, its loss would be more than profound; it would alter consciousness.

Nietzsche wrote that the earliest tragedies had as their sole theme the sufferings of Dionysus. Even when Sophocles or Aeschylus dramatized other tragic heroes such as Oedipus or Prometheus, these figures were "mere masks"[12] of Dionysus. Always operating powerfully beneath the narrative unfolding of the principals' suffering is a deep reenactment of Dionysus's ecstatic unity being violently torn into fragments by the titans. In this original tearing apart Nietzsche sees the enthronement of the principle of *individuation.* With Dionysus's dismemberment, the rapt sense of oneness, of being in communion with all others and with being itself, is lost. The resulting consciousness is particular, cut off, alienated, and in this individuated condition there can be only pessimism and suffering. In this condition only tragic art offers any consolation. For if, as Nietzsche maintained, individuated consciousness is "the primal cause of evil," then art "is the joyous hope that the spell of individuation may be broken in augury of a restored oneness."[13]

But this restoration was not to be. It was, Nietzsche argued, driven back to the darkest recesses of the unconscious by new champions of individuation. The first of these, Nietzsche believed, was Euripides, whose tragedies were shaped and resolved neither by Dionysian nor Apollonian energies, but by a new quality celebrated and lionized by the newly individuated type: *nous,* or wisdom. With the novel, if not always demonstrable, conviction that knowledge might right wrongs and ease suffering, tragic drama, through Euripides, underwent a profound transformation. Forbidden appetite, bloodlust, agony, and suffering were no longer the given conditions of existence; they were assignable consequences for actions known by the gods to be inherently unjust. Euripidean prologues were voiced by knowing figures, sometimes gods, guaranteeing the veracity of what would follow. Moreover, Euripides offered ultimate assurance of rightness prevailing through the dramatic device of the deus ex machina.

With this elevation—in drama and in culture generally—of reasoned wisdom as the ultimate virtue, it would not be long before Dionysus, the intoxicated debunker of all virtues and all restraint, would be identified as archenemy and driven, along with his unmanageable cults, underground.

But even underground, the current of Dionysian fervor could be felt. From a civic, enlightened perspective, Euripides could acknowledge the seductive force of Dionysian desire, but it was a force to be honored gingerly, at a safe distance. It would take an unapologetic hero of reason, Plato's Socrates, to attempt to put Dionysus forever out of human reach.

In Plato's Socratic dialogues, there is no place for Dionysus. Dionysus embodies the negation of reason, considered action, and virtue. For Plato, Socrates lived a life committed to rational discernment of the true from the false, the real from the illusory, the lasting from the temporal, the useful from the useless. The ultimate purpose of life is to live well, and since one cannot live well except as a good citizen in a good polis, life must be dedicated, virtuous, and civic. Any tendencies that might undermine discipline, clarity, and public virtue are destructive of life itself and should therefore be corrected or eliminated altogether.

The Platonic scheme cannot be faulted for lack of clarity—or certainty. In that scheme what Nietzsche called the Dionysian tendency is simply a gross error in human development: the kind of monstrosity to be expected if basic impulses are not channeled and tempered properly by early education.

The educational scheme Plato proposed in *The Republic* is as radically prescriptive as the Dionysian impulse is unrestrained. Like Nietzsche, Plato acknowledges the primal force and original sovereignty of instinctual desire, which Plato calls "the appetites." Unlike Nietzsche, Plato sees no divine genius in the unbounded expression of appetite, only ruinous problems. Thus the first "educational" challenge is to channel the "productive" appetites, to put their energies in reliable service of behavior that will improve the child. Certain "useless" or destructive appetites must be suppressed altogether; these would include any inclination to hilarity, frenzy, cruelty, or unrestrained desire.

Wisdom is revealed in the capacity to *know* that appetites must be tempered to ensure long-term viability. Since such wisdom cannot be expected to arrive until seasoned maturity, the Platonic education to virtue cannot begin didactically, appealing rationally to a not yet arrived capacity to reason. It must begin with—of all things—art. It must begin with stories.

In *The Republic,* Plato's most extended consideration of the relationship between education and virtue, Socrates concedes that art, not reason, must first come to bear on the emerging spirits of children. Children are spirited before they are rational, and their spirits must be engaged by stories. Along with a sensible, moderate program of physical training and music, the educable young must be subjected to stories of a highly specific nature. They must be fictions—but "true fictions" in the manner of fables and parables, which, despite their fantastic situations and characters, teach a moral lesson.

> Our first business will be to supervise the making of fables and legends, rejecting all which are unsatisfactory; and we shall induce nurses and mothers to tell their children only those which we have approved, and to think more of molding their souls with these stories than they do now of rubbing their limbs to make them strong and shapely. Most of the stories now in use must be discarded.[14]

Perhaps grudgingly, Socrates acknowledges in *The Republic* that the fictions selected for the moral training of children cannot deliver their intended impact unless there are also some antagonistic elements or characters. Heroes must be tested by villains. Ants must prove more prudent than grasshoppers, tortoises more dedicated and purposeful than hares. But since spirited children are likely to be as amused and charmed by vivid antagonists as they are by the virtuous heroes, even these moral fictions can pose a problem. The solution proposed in *The Republic* is to censor any suggestion that might cast wrongdoers in a sympathetic or attractive light. And to be safe, Socrates insists that children must recite only the parts of the stories' heroes. The roles of the antagonists would be narrated by the instructor.

> They should from childhood upward, impersonate only the appropriate types of character, men and women who are brave, religious, self-controlled, generous. They are not to do anything mean or dis-

honorable; no more should they be practiced in representing such behavior, for fear of becoming infected with the reality.[15]

For Plato the stories that begin a child's education to virtue are revelatory, not formative. They are intended not to "instill" virtuous conduct but to call such conduct forth from where it lies nascent in some children's souls.

> We must watch them, I think at every age and see whether they are capable of preserving this conviction that they must do what is best for the community, never forgetting it or allowing themselves to be either forced or bewitched into throwing it over.[16]

The children who are instinctively responsive to moral teaching, those most inspired by the stories prescribed in *The Republic,* will in their adolescence be subjected to specially designed tests. Somewhat like the youth of Sparta, they will be assigned missions and challenges by their mentors, exposed unknowingly to every inducement to stray and to indulge selfish desires.

> We must also subject them to ordeals of toil and pain and watch for the same qualities there . . . so these young men must be brought into terrifying situations and then into scenes of pleasure, which will put them to more severe proof than gold tried in a furnace. If we find one bearing himself well in all these trials and resisting every enchantment, preserving always that perfect rhythm and harmony which he has acquired from his training in poetry and music, such a one will be of greatest service to the commonwealth.[17]

Only children who resist temptation and seduction are selected to advance to the next phase of their education as guardians of the Republic.

Throughout the training of these young guardians "art" is cleansed of any appeal to sensual indulgence, to unrestrained feeling of any kind, whether hilarity, grief, or rage. The ecstatic excess celebrated by Nietzsche as the Dionysian tendency is forbidden altogether in the educational plan of *The Republic*. And as dance and music are the surest means of releasing Dionysian feeling, they are strictly regulated.

> We did not want dirges and laments . . . [or] the modes expressing softness and the ones used at drinking parties. . . . Next after the modes will come the principle governing rhythm, which will be, not to aim at a great variety of meters, but to discover the rhythms appropriate to a life of courage and self-control.[18]

In Plato's civic vision, art in either the Dionysian or Apollonian mode is inimical to civil order. In this, Plato is uncompromising. The Gods themselves must comport themselves according to the moral dictates of reason. No longer, it is insisted, should the gods of the pantheon lust adulterously after forbidden partners. Homer's heroic epics, too, should be purged of all traces of their heroes' weaknesses and self-indulgence.

> So we will condemn as a foolish error Homer's description of Zeus as "the dispenser of both good and ill." We shall disapprove if Pandarus' violation of promises and treaties is said to be the work of Zeus and Athena. . . .
>
> Once more then, we shall ask Homer and the other poets not to represent Achilles, the son of a goddess, "tossing from side to side," with all those tears and wailing the poet describes.[19]

Not only should the very heart of Hellenic culture—theogeny, heroic epics, lyric poetry, theater—be cleansed or eradicated, artists themselves should be regarded warily—and when their power of engagement and enchantment poses a threat to civil order, they should be escorted out of the polis. Especially suspect are actors, as they are capable of seeming to be other than they are. Art by its very nature then is deceptive and thus dangerous.

> Suppose, then, that an individual clever enough to assume any character and give imitations of anything and everything should visit our country . . . we shall bow down before such a being . . . , but we shall tell him we are not allowed to have any such person in our commonwealth; we shall crown him with fillets of wool, anoint his head with myrrh, and conduct him to the borders of some other country.[20]

For Nietzsche, art alone enabled the life-giving energy of Dionysus to be expressed and felt in human community. Such art is neither safe nor soothing—and certainly not improving. Nietzsche acknowledged the Athenian achievement of honoring the unthinkable terrors and ecstasies of Dionysus's story through the establishment of a civic monument to pre-civic mystery: the sacred Festival of Dionysus. But no sooner did the genius of tragedy flower than it was held up to the cold, hard light of Socratic reason, its very antithesis and negation.

Dionysus's myth suggests that it is always dangerous and often fatal to oppose or obstruct the god. Thus, as Nietzsche speculated in *The Birth of Tragedy*, the civic maenads of Athens rose up to prosecute and destroy Socrates. Nietzsche felt it was further revelatory that Socrates' last reported dream visitation from his *daimon* concluded in exhortations to work on his art and practice his music.

By enthroning reason as the ruling element over both spirit and appetite in the human soul, Plato's Socrates attempted to establish man's true and best nature. For Socrates reason meets the truth as the eye meets the light of day. No illusion, no caprice, no seductive pleasure must obscure or deflect the rational mind's quest for objective truth. One radical consequence of the enthronement of the rational quest for objective truth is that the gods must go. In Plato's account of Socrates' trial in *The Apology*, Socrates counters his prosecutors' claims that he is impious by leading them into a logical contradiction. He does this first by eliciting their claim that he believes in false gods. Questioning them further, he succeeds in getting one of them to state that he actually believes in no gods whatsoever. At this point he pounces on the logical impossibility of believing simultaneously in false gods and no gods.

This is clever—and to his fellow Athenians annoying—sophistry on Socrates' part, but by revealing a logical contradiction in the claims of his interlocutors, he does not refute what lies at the heart of their second claim: that he does not believe that the gods represent ultimate reality. Indeed in Plato's preceding dialogue, *Euthyphro,* Socrates takes great pains to demonstrate that objective truth commands man's highest allegiance, not gods. Socrates establishes this in the course of a conversation with the Athenian high priest, Euthyphro, who happens to be leaving the courthouse as Socrates is entering it. Immediately Socrates engages Euthyphro, who is presumably an expert, in a discussion of true piety. Socrates proceeds dialectically to reveal a number of contradictions in the answers Euthyphro proposes to his questions. For example, he gets Euthyphro to acknowledge that the gods of the pantheon do contradictory things, such as proscribing adultery and committing adultery. Implicit in this contradiction is the difficulty it poses to those who would honor the gods' intent with respect to adultery and other consequential behavior. As Socrates warms to his task, Euthyphro loses confidence and seems to waver in his certainty. Having won Euthyphro's assent that actions cannot be good simply because gods do them—due to the gods' well-documented contradictory behavior—he gets Euthyphro's agreement that gods do things because those things are inherently good. With this concession, Socrates has managed to establish that there is an eternally reliable, higher standard than the whims of gods, a standard by which the value of gods and their behavior is measured and known—a standard accessible to a disciplined intellect without aid of divine agents.

And so with admirable courtesy and logical precision, Socrates dethrones the gods of the pantheon and with them the theology of desire. "Mathematicians Only" was the slogan engraved over the por-tal of Plato's Academy in Athens. Logic and mathematics along with their material application—science—would define the new philosophic consciousness. In that consciousness nothing exists—even inimically—for which there is no assignable cause or reason. Thus divinity is not merely demoted; it is dispelled—along with, Nietzsche felt, the pulse and exuberance and wonder of life.

> [Socrates'] optimistic dialectic drives music out of tragedy with the scourge of its syllogisms; that is, destroys the essence of tragedy, which can be interpreted only as a manifestation and projection into images of Dionysian states, as the visible symbolizing of music, as the dream-world of a Dionysian intoxication.[21]

Icarus—every child—experiences without the dulling mediation of intellect the pulse and exuberance and wonder of being alive in the world. It might be said of post-Socratic modernity that consciousness has not so much lost its vital pulse and exuberance as it has lost the means, both language and art, to express it. Nietzsche argues that the Socratic achievement and its subsequent science serve to suppress both life-giving Dionysian energy and the beautiful Apollonian illusions—art—that make it endurable.

The only remaining course of existence between the discredited heaven of discredited gods and needless death is the "middle course" of the practical scheme, the course of viable progress through the material world: the real world of Daedalus.

The real world of Daedalus—the Age of Technology—can be seen as the spiritual void created when the Socratic enthronement of rea-son drove the Dionysian life force into forbidden, inaccessible depths. But if, as Nietzsche insists, it *is* a life force and if, however feebly and diminished, we live, then we ought to be able to locate it in some dis-torted or sublimated or displaced form. We might, reasonably, expect to find it as far outside the conventions of applied science as possible, perhaps even in the most ardent or violent negations of applied science: in "countercultural" longing for pretechnical Edens, in antimodern, antidevelopment terrorism, in the celebration of what is most shocking and unintelligible in art, in unapologetic criminality, in the positive celebration of excess, addiction, and insanity.

For youth the stifled, nameless life force is expressed in antiheroics: in the knowing, or at least knowing enough, despair of children who can locate no earthly validation or outlet for what is greatest and sweetest within them, young Hamlets and young Werthes and Holden Caulfields who virtually combust in their agonizing inability to reconcile their worldly circumstances and any will to continue living. Youth so fundamentally bereft and powerless may in compensation assume inflated and fantastic postures. They may build secret arsenals, plot monstrous massacres, don military dress, and make their deadly way to the schoolyard.

Where only the rational is affirmed and named, the irrational—including the deep impulse to worship—tends to make disturbing appearances.

In 1971, the British playwright Peter Shaffer was struck by an anecdote a friend told him in which a disturbed teenage boy put out the eyes of some horses with a hoof pick. His friend did not know the particulars of the crime, nor did Shaffer ever learn them, but something darkly Sophoclean about the incident moved him to write his 1973 play, *Equus*.

The action of the play commences as a ruminative psychiatrist in middle life is asked to take on the treatment of a boy who has put out the eyes of six horses. The psychiatrist, Dysart, nearly declines, since his caseload is already heavy and, more seriously, he has been visited by a growing conviction that his "healing" of troubled youths is in some profound manner destroying their essential vitality. Early in the play he narrates a recent nightmare:

DYSART: That night, I had this very explicit dream. In it I'm a chief
    priest in Homeric Greece. I'm wearing a wide gold mask, all noble

and bearded, like the so-called Mask of Agamemnon found at Mycenae. I'm standing by a thick round stone and holding a sharp knife. In fact, I'm officiating at some immensely important ritual expedition. The sacrifice is a herd of children: about 500 boys and girls. I can see them stretching away in a long queue, right across the plain of Argos . . . on either side of me stand two assistant priests, wearing masks as well: lumpy, pop-eyed masks, such as also were found at Mycenae. They are enormously strong, these other priests, and absolutely tireless. As each child steps forward, they grab it from behind and throw it over the stone. Then, with a surgical skill, which amazes even me, I fit in the knife and slice elegantly down to the navel, just like a seamstress following a pattern. I part the flaps, sever the inner tubes, yank them out and throw them hot and steaming on to the floor. The other two then study the pattern they make, as if they were reading hieroglyphics. It's obvious to me that I'm tops as chief priest. It's this unique talent for carving that has got me where I am. The only thing is, unknown to them, I've started to feel distinctly nauseous.[22]

Dysart's troubling dream is revealing on two counts. First, he is performing those sacred eviscerations as a priest in pre-classical Greek antiquity, the world of Dionysus. In this setting, unlike the reality of his own sterile suburban domesticity, the dramatic pitch of feeling is so powerful as to be unbearable. Second, he now realizes that in performing his sacred duty to the state, he is committing what he is beginning to realize is an abomination: sacrificing the vitality of children on the altar of a false imperative.

Nevertheless, Dysart is a shrewd and effective therapist, and he succeeds first in engaging the boy, Alan, and then in reconstructing the influences and experiences that led him to blind the horses. But in solving the psychiatric riddle and restoring Alan to a functional "normality," Dysart realizes he has sacrificed an ecstatic and vital spark in the boy only to achieve his deadening accommodation to a deadening civic order.

In the course of therapy, Dysart learns how Alan has eroticized and fused a number of contradictions in his largely unhappy lower middle-class household. These sublimated contradictions combine to form an alternative world in which Alan occasionally enacts ecstatic rituals involving horses at a nearby stable. The audience to the play is made to understand how a sequence of horse images and stories and horse-related experiences became fused in Alan's imagination with his mother's intense religiosity to produce an inner world ruled by the divine will of the Horse: Equus.

This process began with the first stories Alan's mother, Dora, read to him. There was the story of Prince, a horse that could only be ridden by one special boy. There were stories of mounted Spanish Conquistadors who appeared to the new world Indians, who had never before seen horses, as fabulous centaurs, the rider and horse appearing to be a single being. Alan's mother also read him the biblical story of Job, including God's lyrical account of the horse's power.

DORA: Hast thou given the horse strength?
    Hast thou clothed his neck with thunder?
    The Glory of his nostrils is terrible!
    He swallows the ground with fierceness and rage!
    He saith among the trumpets—
    Ha! Ha![23]

Dysart learns that Alan's mother had married beneath her class and that both the remembered "equitation" of her girlhood and her desperate religiosity are bitterly resented by her husband. It is further established that Alan's mother and father have unhappily broken off sexual relations, so that Alan's sexual awareness is limited to his mother's vague statements to the effect that sex is not of this world, that it is "higher," "spiritual"—and his atheist father's bitter conclusion that "religion is just bad sex."

When he is twelve and on the brink of pubescence, Alan experiences a formative moment when his father rips down from the wall at the foot of his bed a poster illustrating Christ's agonizing walk bearing his cross to Calvary. Alan's father feels the illustration's chains and whips create a lurid, sadomasochistic effect: "bad sex." Alan is inconsolable at the loss of this picture, which he had purchased himself, until his father hangs a replacement poster in the former spot. The new picture is of a horse's head, its dark eyes staring straight in the direction of the viewer.

Alone in the darkness of his room, held in the stare of the ghostly horse's head, Alan can sometimes be heard chanting fragments of an equine liturgy he has composed. An early school dropout, he works as a clerk in an electronic appliance store. He shows little enthusiasm for his work or for the products the shop sells, but one day a girl tells him he might get a supplementary job tending horses at a stable nearby. He takes the job, and with access now to real horses, he conceives of the ultimate sacrament in his secret faith. Late at night, every three weeks, Alan slips out of his house, unlocks the stable, and prepares a horse, Nugget, for a sacred ride. A number of ritual recitations and actions are performed before Alan strips naked and mounts the horse. As Alan urges Nugget from a trot to a canter, boy and horse ride the perimeter of a dark field until Alan experiences orgasmic release.

ALAN: I'm stiff! Stiff in the wind!
   *My* mane, stiff in the wind!
   My flanks! My hooves!
   . . . I'm raw! Raw!
   Feel me on you! *On* you . . .
   I want to be *in* you!
   I want to BE you forever and ever!
   *Equus,* I *love* you!
   Now!
   Bear me away!
   Make us one person!

*[He rides Equus frantically.]*

One person! One person! One person! One person!
Ha HA! . . . Ha HA! . . . Ha HA![24]

Dysart learns of this nocturnal rite by hypnotizing Alan. The psychiatrist sees no mere pathology in the enactment, but a profound expression of what is missing in his own life—and in that of countless millions of his contemporaries.

As Dysart's analysis of Alan proceeds, he learns that the crime—the blinding—occurred not because of some terrible command generated by the equine gods but because of Alan's unbearable frustration at being unable to reconcile his devotion to them with "real world" claims on his mind and body.

The night of the crime, Alan agrees to accompany a girl on a kind of date, his first. After seeing part of a sexually arousing film—interrupted when Alan spots his father entering the questionable hall—Alan stands up to his father and refuses to go home with him, agreeing instead to accompany Jill to the stable. Though uneasy about entering what is for him a sanctuary, Alan and the girl sneak inside and prepare to make love. Sexually excited but overwhelmed finally by a feeling that he is betraying his gods, Alan is unable to perform the sexual act. At once humiliated, defeated, frightened, and angry, he raises the pick to the eyes of the horses as if to negate their witness of his failed betrayal.

From the perspective of his secret theology, Alan blinded his gods in despair that they had seen his attempted apostasy. Held in the worshipful thrall of such gods, he had sinfully attempted to be "normal." Dysart's therapeutic reenactment allows Alan to purge the terrible tension that had reduced him to delusional hostility at the play's beginning.

At the play's end, Alan is indeed normal, but only in the sense that he will now be fit to serve as a clerk in the appliance store. But this outcome, reassuring from a civic standpoint, requires what Nietzsche and Shaffer might agree is the final denaturing of Alan's spirit.

DYSART: My desire might be to make this boy an ardent husband—a caring citizen—a worshipper of abstract and unifying God. My achievement, however, is more likely to make a ghost!

. . . When that's done, I'll set him on a nice mini-scooter and send him off into the Normal world where animals are treated *properly*: made extinct, put into servitude, tethered all their lives in dim light. . . .

. . . I'll give him the good Normal world. Where we're tethered beside them—blinking our nights away in a non-stop drench of cathode ray over our shriveling heads! I'll take away his field of Ha Ha, and give him Normal places for his ecstasy—multi-lane highways driven through the guts of cities. . . . He'll trot his metal pony tamely through the concrete evening—and one thing I will promise you: he will never touch hide again! With any luck his private parts will come to feel as plastic to him as the products of the factory to which he will be almost certainly sent. Who knows? He may even come to find sex funny . . . I *doubt, however, with much passion!*[25]

Shaffer has Dysart conclude the play with the grim suggestion that the Normality awaiting Alan is modern consciousness itself. That world is not a world without wonders of a kind. There is, for example, television: that "non-stop drench of cathode-ray over our shriveling heads." There is also the multilane highway, the miniscooter, the factory, the appliance shop where Alan stood at the counter dispensing all the modern fabrications of Daedalus: "Philco, Remington, Robex, Croydex, Volex, Pifco, Hoover. . . ."

The Normality of contemporary life may indeed reside in the creation and exchange of material conveyances and gadgets and toys. Daedalus is everywhere about, fashioning wings. But are there still signs of Icarus, rapt in his play, not paying attention, secretly waiting, as Alan waited, for heaven's call?

# 4

## ICARUS EMBODIED

*The Puer Spirit in Real Lives*

DAEDALUS TOILS WITH great skill and great determination to fashion working wings so that he and his boy can escape his sentence of confinement to Crete. He has a plan, a scheme; he knows exactly what he is doing. Icarus, if he is even aware of the escape plan, takes no interest in it. He is bored by the work, wants only to play. In these opposed intentions, Daedalus and Icarus are every father and every son, every responsible adult, every spirited child.

The "acculturation" of such children is the central, educative task of civilization. There will be no civic future unless youth can be somehow made to forsake immediate delight and the spirit of play for disciplined work: for the "middle course" of livable accommodation. We are fully and intuitively aware of the dramatic tension between Daedalus and Icarus. They are father and son, but their deepest inclinations are opposed. There is inherent trouble and danger in this opposition. The irreconcilability of their types is both comic and potentially tragic. It never fails to interest us.

The inherent tension between fathers and beloved sons is an archetypal story. The working out of the problem continues to shape the history of civilization. The drama unfolds in every household; for every son is at heart, for a time, a prodigal son, whether playfully impervious, rebellious, or unreachably dreamy. The Christian parable of the prodigal son—which some interpreters prefer to call the parable of the loving father—is an attempt to show a viable resolution of the problem. The prodigal of the parable is a *younger* son, one saved by birth order from the cultural necessity of bending his neck prematurely to the adult responsibilities that will extinguish his puer spirit. The prodigal son does not agonize over his decision to take off and experience the world ecstatically. He is not fearful of losing the security and comforts of home and civil order—because he was born to that condition. Comfort and safety are not earned or learned; they are his birthright. He goes on to squander his paternal inheritance in passing delights and in sensual excesses until his reduced circumstances indenture him to tend pigs for a hard master in an alien land. When he realizes he would rather be a servant in his father's household than to continue to toil for subsistence from a stranger, he resolves in a burst of humility to return home. The resolution here is both surprising and joyful. The father no sooner is apprised of his lost son's approach, than he calls for a great feast of celebration. Over his dutiful first born son's objection that no such honor has ever been conferred on him, the father tells him that he has always enjoyed his father's preferments and blessings. The prodigal, by contrast, was lost and now regained. Such a restoration can only be celebrated. There is no afterward in the parable. One is left with the suggestion that both sons have learned something profound about the value of loving paternity. The elder son was unflaggingly dutiful; the prodigal through error and suffering and penitence has learned to be likewise. The returning prodigal is no longer a puer spirit, although his father does not know this when he joyfully welcomes him back. Implicit in the story is the assumption that in the crucible of alienation and hardship, the puer spirit is somehow shed, transformed into mature adaptive acceptance of personal responsibility in the adult order.

The motif of the redemption of spirited boys through suffering and penitence can also be seen in the biblical accounts of the Hebrew patriarchs and kings. Jacob, the younger twin of Isaac, deliberately cheats his brother Esau out of his inheritance and birthright, only to be banished in fear to a desolate wilderness. Taken in later by a prosperous uncle, Jacob himself is deceived unfairly when his sister-in-law Leah is substituted in disguise for his expected bride, Rachel. It would take an additional seven years of hard labor to win his intended love. Later, fleeing from his disaffected uncle with no safe homeland to return to, he experiences a transforming encounter with an angel, with whom he wrestles one dark night, emerging from the combat with a pelvic injury. But because he has contended and endured, he is divinely renamed "Israel," *he who struggles with God.*

Joseph, the younger darling of Jacob's sons, undergoes a similar sequence of trials and suffering before being elevated to mature, accomplished patriarchy. The charmed adolescent David, fearless slayer of the Philistine giant Goliath and soon after a celebrated favorite in King Saul's household, is unfairly vilified, exiled, hunted down as if a criminal. David, too, contends and suffers—emerging wily, disillusioned, and deliberate. A great king, a warrior, a national founder, he is also, as his calculated adultery with Bathsheba reveals, fallible, a sinner, a sufferer of consequences, far, far from his puer spirit.

In the biblical narratives, to live in the puer spirit presages error and suffering. The alternatives are to grow past it or to perish. The historical record is replete with such perishing—for not all beloved heirs are capable of forsaking the puer spirit. On this point the tumultuous succession of Roman emperors is instructive. The early imperial historian Tacitus writes of the tragic consequences of attempting to pass on the responsibilities and authority of rule to beloved sons, especially when the sons are still held in the puer spirit. The imperial record makes a stunning case that the puer spirit politically enthroned is catastrophic for the established order. The youthful emperor Gaius, nicknamed Caligula ("Little Boots") by the soldier comrades of his general father, Germanicus, because of the child's habit of parading about in soldiers' boots, is the first of several boy emperors whose unrestrained whims and indulgences in office brought the imperium to near collapse. As a child, Caligula was a charmed darling of his noble family and a kind of mascot to his father's troops. Elevated to the divine status of Augustus when barely past adolescence, his desire knew no practical limit. He commanded ruinously expensive spectacles, directed police to strike, and legions to campaign at his capricious will. Apparently he did not experience his divine status as emperor on any symbolic or abstractly metaphysical level. He felt he *was* divine. He was seen to whisper into the ear of the statues of the gods. He carried with him silver facsimiles of lightning bolts that he would hurl clatteringly onto the cobblestones of the forum—sentencing to death any who laughed. He once had the Roman fleet tethered together into a floating bridge across the mouth of the Tiber at Ostia to demonstrate that he could walk on water. When these unworldly projections had sufficiently offended the *gravitas* of the ruling order and when they had seriously depleted the treasury reserves of the empire, Caligula was murdered by the Praetorian Guard.

The internal regicide of Caligula did not, however, solve the generational problems of the early empire. The internecine scheming of the Augustan nobility would give rise to the excesses of Nero and subsequent civil strife before the second century emperors decreed an end to hereditary succession in favor of a system of "adoptive succession" in which proven statesmen and guards would be formally adopted by the reigning emperor. This period of relative stability and prosperity prevailed over the final century of what the Greco-Roman world would call the Pax Romana, before a close succession of internal dislocations and peripheral troubles would cause the imperial structure to disintegrate altogether. Tellingly, this disintegration was triggered by another ill-starred gesture on the part of a loving father for a headstrong son.

It was Marcus Aurelius no less, the stoic philosopher and last emperor of the Pax Romana, who put aside the adoptive succession rule in favor of his own notorious son, Commodus. Like Caligula and Nero before him, Commodus soon offended both noble and popular sensibilities by reckless excesses and public displays of personal vanity, and he, too, was murdered by the guard.

Even in the following century, dominated by a succession of soldier emperors and beset by internal division and invasions at the empire's borders, something in the collective Roman spirit seemed to long for the ethereal vitality of the puer. Indeed, sustained warfare and economic depression create a promising climate for the irrational exuberance of a puer-redeemer. Such seems to have been the case with the brief elevation in the third century of the boy-emperor Elagabalus (sometimes written Heliogabalus).

Elagabalus was fourteen years old when he was named Emperor. A distant relative of the brutal soldier-emperor Caracalla, Elagabalus had no political experience whatsoever. Raised in Syria as a priest of the cult of Baal, Elagabalus cut a novel figure among his new subjects. As historian Robert Payne writes, he was, among other things, promiscuously pansexual. "[H]e found pleasure in dressing in women's clothes and posing as a prostitute; he had a fondness for walking on carpets of lilacs and roses."[1]

A contemporary historian, Herodian, describes Elagabalus's inaugural procession into the capital draped in purple silk embroidered with gold. His face was vividly rouged and his eyes darkened as he made his way flanked by elaborately arrayed oriental priests and eunuchs. In the four years of his rule (before being murdered in a latrine and thrown into the Tiber) he briefly installed the practice of Baal worship in Rome. He insisted on furnishings of gold and silver and studded the wheels of his chariots with precious gems. He would bathe only in pools scented with saffron. His eccentric banquets would feature meals of a single sensational color—blue, emerald, iridescence. He himself favored peacock tongue and ostrich brains. He was a prankster who was known to install lions and bears in the sleeping chambers of his guests. He offered a bounty to the servant who could bring him a thousand pounds of spider webs. Late at night he was known to walk the streets of the capital incognito, slipping coins into the hands of prostitutes, with the whispered message: "a gift from your emperor." And while he would ultimately appall the senate and magistrates of Rome, his outrageous appearance and antics helped to make him, for a time, a popular darling, a figure somehow able to defy the crushing weight of imperial business.

Whether viewed historically or experienced personally, the beloved boy—even the favored boy, even the fervid hope of a boy-redeemer—is a problem. Some of the problem may lie in the belovedness itself.

The historical record and the vast literature of coming-of-age stories worldwide suggest that the boy must shed his puer spirit or he will perish. The passage in which this shedding must be accomplished is a rite or ordeal of some kind. To be definitive it must be no less than life threatening. To suffer, to be wounded in the ordeal is essential. Jungian and other psychoanalytic writers insist that there must be a separation and liberation from mothers if boys are to become fully individuated as men. Mothers by nature resist the separation. For them the endangering, wounding, and suffering of sons are intolerable. Again, seen this way, a boy's deepest needs and his mother's deepest needs—which together compose the culture's deepest needs—are irreconcilable: a problem.

The medieval legend of Percival is an archetypal telling of a boy's progress into manhood. The story is explicated with great compassion and clarity in Robert Johnson's study, *He*. The boy is born, as his name Percival/Parsifal suggests, a "little fool." Unbeknownst to him, he is the youngest son of a family of medieval knights, all of whom have been killed in combat. His mother, Heart's Sorrow, determines that Percival will not be lost in this manner, so she sets up a household with him in a remote cottage in a secluded forest, far from the influence of men and their causes and wars. But as Percival grows into boyhood, he reveals an instinctive inclination for martial arts—specifically, whittling sticks to an approximation of javelins, which he learns to thrust with force and accuracy. Then one day he spots in a clearing a party of mounted knights, the sun gleaming on their armor. Reared only on scripture and other pieties from his mother, Percival does not know who these soul-stirring beings could be, and he concludes that they must be angels. When he reports this wonderful discovery to his mother, she senses that this son, too, must depart, and she sews him some homespun clothes and lets him take the family nag on what will be his personal quest to become an angel/knight. Before Percival departs, his mother tells him of the necessity to worship regularly and that he must always honor women. Because he is impulsive and foolish—because he is a boy—he quickly forgets, or confuses, these instructions, much as Jack forgets and confuses his mother's instructions to sell the family cow at a good price in "Jack and the Beanstalk."

But the puer spirit once liberated is, at least for a spell of time, charmed and often irresistible. Against all likelihood, Percival makes his way to King Arthur's court, manages to engage a menacing Red Knight in mortal combat and, again improbably, prevails. Donning the fallen knight's armor (although still wearing his mother's homespun under-neath) and assuming a proper mount, Percival is on his way to becoming a true knight, a real man. On this journey he will engage in a series of familiar archetypal experiences. He will study with a wise mentor, rescue a damsel, forego lust, have an intimation of divine integration (a vision of the grail), fail to understand it, wander aimlessly, suffer. As Percival proceeds, he grows painfully conscious. The earliest medieval texts of the Percival legend trail off inconclusively. There does not seem to be a coherent or satisfying ending. What is clear, however, is that Percival grows past Heart's Sorrow's devotion to him. It is also clear that, once he is frustrated by his failure to understand his vision of the grail and begins to wonder and to doubt, he is no longer connected to his puer spirit.

Marie-Louise von Franz proposes in her study of *Puer Aeternus* that conscription into armed service is a modern collective solution by which the puer can be helped to grow out of his mother complex. It might be said also that a young man's assumption into the cold, profit-driven machinations of the industrial economy serve a similar tie-breaking function. But there is also a clearly chartable resistance on the part of youth to conscription into either service. Rousseau's autobiographical *Confessions* and his romantic evocation of a child's "natural" education, *Emile,* can be seen as an eighteenth century call to recognize the primacy of the individual spirit—beginning with its bright unfolding in childhood—over the civic constructs of the state and its commerce. As mechanization and industrialization added new dimensions of weight and constraint to urban life in the West, puer resistance would increase dramatically. The poems in William Blake's *Songs of Innocence and of Experience* sound both prophetic and nostalgic notes as they dramatize the tension between the lost world of the puer and the hellish military-industrial reality of late-eighteenth-century London.

> *I wander thro' each charter'd street*
> *Near where the charter'd Thames does flow.*
> *And mark in every face I meet*
> *Marks of weakness, marks of woe.*
>
> *In every cry of every Man*
> *In every infant's cry of fear,*
> *In every voice, in every ban,*
> *The mind-forged manacles I hear.*
>
> *How the chimney-sweeper's cry*
> *Every blackening Church appalls,*
> *And the hapless Soldier's sigh*
> *Runs in blood down Palace walls.*
>
> *But most through midnight streets I hear*
> *How the youthful Harlot's curse*
> *Blasts the new-born infant's tear,*
> *And blights with plagues the Marriage hearse.*

In this grimy, spoiled world the bright dreams of the puer are blackened as faces and lungs of boy chimney sweeps were blackened by the deadly conditions of that work.

*When my mother died I was very young,*
*And my father sold me while yet my tongue*
*Could scarcely cry "'weep! 'weep! 'weep! 'weep!"*
*So your chimneys I sweep, & in soot I sleep.*

For children conscripted to such toxic toil, the only redemption was in a world to come: a redemption into sweetness, into eternal childhood.

*Then naked and white, all their bags left behind,*
*They rise upon clouds, and sport in the wind;*
*And the Angel told Tom, if he'd be a good boy,*
*He'd have God for his father and never want joy.*

Decades later Blakes "charter'd streets" would be evoked vividly in Dickens' coming-of-age classics, *Great Expectations, Oliver Twist, David Copperfield,* and *Nicholas Nickleby.* Terrible injustices and privations befall the boy protagonists, and the most ruthless of these blows are delivered by those who would in the name of public or commercial necessity foreshorten the happiness of spirited children. The Dickens protagonists are able to survive their passage through their respective privations and cruelties only through fortuitous interventions or pastoral escapes. There is the saving presence of lovable but childlike adult picaresques. There is an occasional rescue by infinitely wise and caring mother and father figures. The Dickensian child-hero is either a virtual or actual orphan. His value lies in his inalienable child spirit, not his hard won virtue. Although Pip and Oliver and David make their episodic progress from sweet childhood to accomplished young manhood, there is no tenable suggestion that such progression is essential or even improving. Indeed, in Dickens' *Christmas Carol,* which encompasses the coming of age motifs of the novels and depicts the complete male cycle from early childhood to advanced old age, there is no suggestion whatever that "innocence" will in the right conditions ripen into "experience." Instead, Scrooge steadily worsens as he passes from the dreams and caprices of his childhood into the confinements of commerce and practical survival. The Christmas Eve ghosts that visit him restore him first to childhood, then to a hellish vision of that childhood forsaken. His fervent wish upon awakening from his vision of death and meaninglessness is to restore the vitality of a crippled boy, Tiny Tim.

There would be no abatement in mechanization, industrialization, and urbanization as the world of Dickens proceeded into the twentieth century and its two great wars. The technics that derived first from steam compression and then from internal combustion, the mass refinement of steel, which enabled, among other things, the erection of urban skyscrapers, changed forever the common human landscape, the landscape of memory and imagination. There were and still are wild places, bucolic places, pastoral places, but the industrial advance has been accompanied by a mounting collective sense—or dread—that such places are mere preserves, soon to become organic museums in a relentless, all-encompassing industrial order.

In his study of late-nineteenth- and early-twentieth-century children's literature, *Secret Gardens,* Humphrey Carpenter sees in such stories as *Alice in Wonderland, Peter Pan, Wind in the Willows,* and *Winnie the Pooh* a hearkening back to an unspoiled vernal world in which a child's spirit can fully live.

The settings of these fictions are pre-industrial, pastoral, Arcadian. They are emphatically Never Never Lands, in that elements of the industrial, urban order are only incorporated—as Mr. Toad's motorcar is incorporated in *Wind and the Willows*—as a cautionary example of how the golden world of pure child sensibility can go wrong. Carpenter suggests that in such refound arcadias, in such secret gardens, children are able to locate their true spirit.

# 5

## ICARUS IN THE MODERN WORLD

*The Case of Antoine de Saint-Exupéry*

IF IMAGINATIVE EVOCATIONS of secret gardens allow the puer spirit free expression, the appearance on the world stage of actual, uncompromised puer-spirited beings can be even more exhilarating. Such seems to have been the case with the French aviator and writer, Antoine de Saint-Exupéry.

Saint-Exupéry was an in-this-world, twentieth-century historical figure whose life seems to have been largely unbounded by practical, worldly constraints of any kind.

Saint-Exupéry was puer spirit writ large. He was born in 1900 into the sumptuous but fast receding world of French landed nobility, his family title dating back to the medieval crusades. He was the third child and firstborn son of Jean and Marie de Saint-Exupéry.

Well born but not really well off, Jean de Saint-Exupéry worked briefly as an inspector for an insurance firm before dying prematurely of a stroke when Antoine was four. While Antoine's, or "Tonio's," father was only a shadowy figure in the child's early life, his mother was central, a vivid and adored presence for as long as he lived. For the first six years of his life, Tonio's head was covered with golden curls, which inspired his mother to call him "the sun king." He delighted in the title and for a time carried a miniature green throne around the house, settling himself into it wherever his mother came to rest.

The world into which Saint-Exupéry was born was both enchanted castle and secret garden. It was the country estate, the chateau Saint-Maurice-de-Rémens forty-five miles south of Lyons. Later, Antoine would recall this as "the secret kingdom," the "interior world of roses and fairies." The polished parlors, meandering passages and opulent gardens and grounds of the chateau composed an order in which little Tonio felt not only at home but providentially placed. Like the subject and title of his most famous book, St. Exupéry felt he was forever a little prince. The first passion of his life, storytelling, found expression when the Saint-Exupérys were rusticated for the summer months at Saint-Maurice-de-Rémens.

As a young man and afterward until his death in 1944, St. Exupéry alternated erratically between flamboyant extroversion and tortured shyness—but as a boy he was exuberant in his play, wildly imaginative, and imperious. Young Tonio liked to listen to stories read to him, especially those of Jules Verne and Hans Christian Anderson, but he soon grew impatient to tell and then to write his own. Later his family would recall his habit of concocting a story well past his bedtime, then rousing his mother and siblings for a command recital. An aunt observed, "he was a first-rate devil."

At school he was bright, easily distracted, inclined to mischief and lapses into reverie. It was in the years of his preadolescent schooling that he became obsessed with the workings of motors and engines, an obsession that would soon after embrace the technics of flight. Tonio was scolded for "boring" his relatives with insistent questions about the operation of engines. For a time he was transfixed by the present of a small hot-oil motor, but he was forced to give it up when it exploded in his little brother's face. By the time he was twelve he had designed a flying bicycle, which extruded a rigging of wings made from bed sheets. Family remembered Tonio pedaling furiously, attempting to lift his craft airborne. The result was usually torn clothing and bloodied knees—prefiguring the string of crashes that would mark his career as a flyer.

Mme. Saint-Exupéry and her children were supported in reasonable comfort by sympathetic relatives, but they had no real means or inheritance of their own. The acquisition of money, possessions, and a settled place to live would vex and bewilder St. Exupéry throughout his life. Impatient of business, businessmen, and indeed "administration" of any kind, he would become an inveterate spendthrift, a shameless borrower, and a guiltless holder of bad debt. As an adult, he would live without complaint in comfortless shacks on remote Saharan air stations, in nicely appointed flats in New York and Paris, in commodious country cottages, and in featureless hotel rooms. After the sale and liquidation of the furnishings of Saint-Maurice-de-Rémens, Saint-Exupéry drifted from continent to continent, climate to climate, temporary residence to temporary residence without a settled home.

By the time he was a young man, the seemingly unconnected elements in St. Exupéry's life began to cohere in a pattern that would define the rest of his life. He would career about, scanning his experience for stories. He would find those stories in the challenges and romance of early aviation. Then he would seek out sympathetic women who would unconditionally adore him, women to whom he could tell his stories. His most popular published books and journalism tended to be short in length, melodramatic and romantic in tone. All of his books were memoirs or fictionalized memoirs of flight—except his late eccentric work, *The Little Prince*. *The Little Prince* is narrated in the voice of a flyer who, like Saint-Exupéry, once crashed a plane in the Sahara. The aviator is visited by a gnomic, charming little prince who has fallen to earth from a distant planet and who is seeking in a seemingly childlike way to answer the questions of life's meaning. The tale begins fantastically and whimsically with something of the freshness and eccentricity Christopher Robin conveys in *Winnie the Pooh*. But the little prince moves from playful illogic to serious existential concerns, such as giving beloved persons their due and finding the fortitude to continue living.

Even before Saint-Exupéry reached his full adult stature, he realized he had grown quite big. He would prove to be—especially for a flyer—a large and often awkward figure, prone to minor and major accidents, continually bumping his head while ducking into cars or under other low overhangs. The family of a young woman he ardently courted referred to him out of hearing as "the vague pachyderm." When he was in his thirties, he confessed to his wife that he still felt a little boy with blond curls, "but I am bald, quite bald."

Photographs of Saint-Exupéry as a child reveal a nicely formed little boy. His head is decidedly large, his face both intelligent and appealing under a corona of curly hair. His dark eyes are large and look into the camera with an intelligent intensity. With the exception of his eyes, it is hard to see any continuity of these boyhood features in the adult photographs. He would grow to be a big man, six feet and a few inches. Daring, active, but never really fit, he would assume by the time he was twenty a bearlike, bulky stature. As he remarked himself in some wonder, his hair grew thin and patchy on his pate. He was a heavy smoker and a tireless drinker, and these habits, combined with the accrued batterings his body suffered as a result of his crashes, make him appear at forty-four, the year he and his plane disappeared, bloated and spent, old beyond his years. But photographs cannot always capture essential qualities, such as lilt and exuberance. There are photographs of Saint-Exupéry smiling, but they do not suggest the impression of his good friend Léon-Paul Fargue, who wrote that Saint-Exupéry "left permanent wounds in the hearts of those who saw him smile, even once." His flying comrades, nonreaders who were largely unaware of his literary reputation, remember the young Saint-Exupéry as "unforgettable," a presence they immediately sensed as "very big and very famous."

From his infancy onward Saint-Exupéry was an infectious and compulsive storyteller. The little boy who would wake up his mother, brother, and sisters in the middle of the night and insist they listen to a new tale he had conceived would continue a pattern of rapt storytelling throughout his adult life. He had dozens of life-threatening crashes, accidents, and narrow escapes to recount, and he was equally fascinated by such mishaps on the part of his friends and fellow flyers. An uninterruptible raconteur in cafes and bistros and barracks mess halls, his best stories, the ones that would inspire his flight books, told of being lost and disoriented in impossible flying conditions: winds and storms that overpowered the plane's mechanical capacity, absolute loss of vision and the feeling of total disorientation in black space, the partial or complete failure of the plane's engine and body. The feeling of being closer to the stars—both physically and emotionally—than to the departed earth below was a strong motif in Saint-Exupéry's published work.

While aloft and in such danger himself, Saint-Exupéry admitted to feeling as he did when he was a small boy in the darkness of his bedroom in Saint-Maurice-de-Rémens. Haunted by Jules Verne tales of life in deep darkness, darkness under the surface of the earth, underneath the sea, he longed to see, to find a way past darkness, to immerse himself happily in a world of luminous, lovely stars. This is of course the home, the world from which Saint-Exupéry's *Little Prince* would descend. This final, beckoning nighttime of stars that transcends all earthly catastrophes was likened in Saint-Exupéry's mind to the heavenly sense of well-being he experienced when his mother would come to his darkened bedside and lovingly smooth the sheets with her hands.

The fascination with which Saint-Exupéry was beheld grew out of the stunning paradox he represented. On one hand, he needed to rise above or otherwise resist the working world by open resistance, daydreaming, mischief, or sustained inattention—while at the same time embracing highly specific elements of that reality, incorporating them into stories that allowed him to shape, in a godlike way, his distinctive picture of the world. All through his early and adolescent school years, he considered himself chiefly a writer, a poet. A precocious reader of great moderns such as Dostoevsky, Baudelaire, and Mallarmé, Saint-Exupéry maintained a conviction that as long as he could create stories, he would not have to bow to the unendurable tedium of the given world. In his final years as a *lycée* student, although his school specialized in applied sciences, Saint-Exupéry spent most of his time sketching and versifying. He won recognition only for his artwork. He would later fail the examination for admission to the École Navale (the equivalent of the U.S. Naval Academy at Annapolis), but while enrolled in preparatory classes in Paris, he had a revealing encounter with the Catholic school authorities.

The Lycée Saint Louis was set up so that most of the scholars studied at long tables along which they shared seats on common benches. There were also a few much-prized desks in the rear of the hall, which offered storage space for personal effects and also the comfort of individual chairs. For some reason Saint-Exupéry was given one of the special desks, which he treasured. But as had been the case with his previous work stations at school—and with all of his living quarters before and afterward—Antoine quickly and openly made a huge mess of the desk area, with scraps of paper, drawings, unsorted and personal effects littering surfaces, shelves, drawers. The Abbé who supervised these study halls warned Antoine repeatedly to clean up his desk, but Saint-Exupéry failed to do it, so that one day quite suddenly he lost his desk and was assigned to the common benches and tables. Not conventionally rebellious but nevertheless unable to bear this loss of special privilege, Saint-Exupéry surprised his fellow scholars and the Abbé by inscribing, without invitation, a poem of complaint on the chalkboard.

> *I sat in the back, to the side,*
> *A desk hardly worth a dollar,*
> *Yet I was like a badge of pride*
> *To my illustrious owner,*

*Black as a native of the tropics,*
*Worn down by years of bleakest tasks,*
*I was, prudent and pacific,*
*By far the most serene of desks.*

*Well positioned by the window,*
*Sunning myself like a lizard,*
*I was endowed by my master*
*With disorder, approaching art.*
*Our serenity was profound.*
*Nothing troubled our staid repose.*
*We were more sheltered from the world*
*Than the happy dead in their tombs.*

*Any wish I might have expressed*
*Was confined to the status quo.*
*But my peace was evanescent.*
*And I, old hunk of rococo,*
*Was banished from this perfect calm.*

*Like a king, I was driven out,*
*To molder in another room,*
*O my dear master, far from thou.*

*ENVOI*
*You, who in a single motion,*
*Denied all our good protests,*
*Please, touched by this petition,*
*Do return to me my little desk.*[1]

Upon seeing this impertinent, if elegant, entreaty on the board, the Abbé demanded that it be removed at once. But before it was erased, a friend of Saint-Exupéry's transcribed the poem in his notebook, taking pains to show it to the Abbé later in his study. The whimsical charm of the petition ultimately softened the instructor's heart. He relented and reassigned Antoine to his beloved desk.

This anecdote reveals another recurring motif in Saint-Exupéry's life: the acknowledgment by instructors, accreditors, officers, employers, that Saint-Exupéry was an exception to standard policy and to ordinary expectations. Even in his required military service to follow, he would not turn himself out in standard uniform, nor were his bunk and quarters ever in order. While in the service, he managed to maintain his own off-base flat for more comfortable and restorative pastimes than military life could possibly offer. Indeed, Saint-Exupéry never quite dressed for occasion, nor would he ever keep his personal effects, including the haphazard scraps of paper on which he composed his books, in any coherent order.

Yet he was in no way an attention-demanding egotist. Neither prima donna nor *enfant terrible*, he was more often quite taciturn, a self-effacing bear of a young man, shambling along on the margins of instructional activity. In his late teens and early twenties, he would quietly accept the teasing of his friends about his clumsiness, oafish appearance, his "trumpetlike" nose. In an elusive manner his friends could not quite name, Saint-Exupéry was not really a "type" at all. He was unique—and he was, again, unforgettable to those who encountered him.

Having failed to gain entry to the Naval School, Saint-Exupéry enrolled in the École des Beaux-Arts in Paris where, in a desultory way, he "studied" architecture for a year. Living languorously and rather sumptuously in a relative's commodious apartment, Saint-Exupéry wondered what was to become of him. He could not, for a spell, locate a story that felt worthy of him. A friend and fellow artist at Beaux-Arts described Saint-Exupéry at twenty:

A strange thing: this big man, this gentleman of such impressive size . . . had in fact the sensibility of a little girl. It was bizarre; the two didn't go together. He was very sensitive, kind, and always a bit awkward.[2]

What his friend could not seem to find the words to say is that at twenty, the hulking presence of Saint-Exupéry was somehow sheer puer spirit—an uncompromised boy. The boy-spirited Saint-Exupéry would find fuller expression as his capacity for story-making found its subject in the beauty and terror of flight.

Saint-Exupéry and modern aviation came of age together. In 1903, when Antoine was three, the Wright Brothers would sustain a brief flight over a clearing at Kitty Hawk, North Carolina. The wonder of the feat did not impress the United States or British war departments sufficiently to offer to buy the celebrated invention. The French, however, were more sympathetic, and in 1908 the Wrights licensed their craft, the Flyer, to a French syndicate in Le Mans where the brothers set up shop. Their demonstration flights in 1908 and 1909 awed and delighted growing throngs of spectators. The Saint-Exupérys moved to Le Mans in 1909 to school the children, and while Tonio would arrive too late to observe the Flyer's airborne circuits, he would inhale the very atmosphere of early flight.

When Saint-Exupéry was born, the airplane had not yet been invented. By the time he was fourteen, early planes had crossed the English Channel, flown nonstop from capital to capital, carried the first airmail, and performed aeronautical acrobatics. Women pilots made their debut at the controls—and some perished. There were not only fatal crashes, but midair collisions. Prize money was put up for the first transatlantic flight, the fastest flight around the world.

All of this was thrilling to Tonio. From his summer idyll at Saint-Maurice-de-Rémens, he would bicycle to a newly opened airstrip nearby where Lyonnais investors were trying out new metal-bodied planes designed by the Polish Wrobleski brothers. Tonio haunted the hangars and hounded the mechanics about technical details. His most insistent request was that he be allowed to be taken along on a flight. He was twelve at the time—the age Christ surprised the elders in the temple by discoursing learnedly on religious questions. Tonio also badgered his mother to go with him to the airfield, with the intention of getting her permission for him to be taken aloft. Madame Saint-Exupéry understandably forbade any such notion, but one day in July 1912, Antoine succeeded in putting one over on Gabriel Wrobleski, the designer and pilot of the new Berthoud-W metal planes. As chronicled later by a young mechanic, Saint-Exupéry addressed Wrobleski as follows:

—Sir, maman has now authorized me to receive my baptism.
—Is that true?
—Yes, sir, I promise you![3]

The fib succeeded and Antoine was taken aboard for two circuits over the airfield. A young friend of Tonio's who witnessed the adventure reported that Saint-Exupéry "jumped for joy"[4] upon resuming the ground. From that point forward his talk, even his early flirting, was full of aeronautical tall tales. He penned a poem for his teacher at school that began:

*The wings quivered in the evening breeze*
*The engine's song lulled the sleeping soul.*

A year and a half later both Wrobleski brothers were killed when their Berthoud crashed on that very airstrip. Mme. Saint-Exupéry insisted that a condolence letter from Tonio accompany her own.

It would be another ten years before Antoine, in the course of fulfilling his required military service, would become himself a licensed flyer. His flight training was eccentric to the point of irresponsibility. He was stationed in Strasbourg where he had selected a posting in aviation. But while there were a number of alluring planes on the airfield, Strasbourg was not a flight-training center for pilots. Only those who had already secured civilian licenses were allowed to train. The likely course for the decidedly unmartial Saint-Exupéry was either as a gunner or ground crew. But at such a prospect he drew uncharacteristically on class and family connections. He was, after all, the *Comte* de Saint-Exupéry.

That there was no flight training course officially offered at the Strasbourg base made it especially remarkable that Saint-Exupéry, inefficient and oblivious in so many other respects, found a way. He persuaded his base commander to allow him to train during off-duty hours with an instructor from a civilian flight company specializing in aerial photography and pleasure rides. The conditions of this arrangement were that no official mention or photographs of the flight sessions were to be made. Authorization for such a venture had never before been granted. To his mother, who was asked to put up the considerable cost of his tuition, Antoine wrote, "I beg you mother, do not speak of this to *anyone*."[5]

In his first lesson in the dual-controlled plane, Saint-Exupéry circled the airfield three times and landed three times. His instructor urged him to be "less brutal" with the controls. Two weeks, eleven lessons, and twenty-one circuits later, on July ninth of his twenty-first year, Saint-Exupéry and his teacher completed a circuit and landed the craft. His teacher then exited the cockpit and ordered Saint-Exupéry to take off. Saint-Exupéry was incredulous. He had logged a total of two-and-a-half hours in the air. The solo ascent and circuit went flawlessly, but the young pilot overaccelerated as he neared the ground, causing the engine to backfire before catching again. Safely if imperfectly landed, Saint-Exupéry was told to make another circuit, which he completed satisfactorily. When Saint-Exupéry's solo was reported to the base commander, it was determined on the spot that the course of instruction was completed.

The following year Saint-Exupéry managed to pass the requisite exams and was licensed as a pilot. Bored and impatient with the tedium of military life, he continued to sketch and to write verses. At this time he was also remembered as a master of sensational card tricks, an accomplishment that would engage him and appreciative observers for the rest of his life. His *ennui* led to recklessness one morning when

Saint-Exupéry decided to treat a fellow second lieutenant to a joyride in an airfield outside of Paris. The plane he selected was a craft he was not trained to fly. A minute after taking off, the plane went into a spin at about three hundred feet and crashed to the ground. The plane was mangled, his friend suffered a fractured skull, and Saint-Exupéry was badly bruised all over his body. The accident had been his fault, but he would write about the crash and his survival to his mother with airy nonchalance. Because his superiors had found him otherwise an excellent pilot—"made to be a flyer,"—he was only lightly disciplined and temporarily grounded for his misadventure.

While the appearance of his books would later make him a very famous flyer, Saint-Exupéry may not ever have been a greatly skilled one. When in his midtwenties he landed a job as an early airmail pilot, the plane he flew most successfully was a Breguet 14, a biplane designed for military use and purchased by the pioneering Latécoère Company for mail service. The Breguet 14 was simple, sturdy, and slow. While its cruising speed rarely exceeded 80 mph, it could fly for thousands of miles without mechanical breakdown. Breguets landed safely with broken wings, damaged pistons. They were unheated, open cockpit planes, with few instruments, no compass, no headlights. It would be in a Breguet that Exupéry was assigned his first mail flight round trip from Toulouse to Alicante, Spain. Crossing the Pyrenees even in favorable weather was precarious, as the Breguet could not sustain altitudes of over thirteen thousand feet. Visibility was often poor, and there were no opportunities for emergency landing. Saint-Exupéry took off on his first southern run in heavy rain but safely crossed the mountains and alighted first in Barcelona, then Alicante, which delighted him for being the only city in Europe "warm enough for dates to ripen." On the return to Toulouse he once again managed the Pyrenees crossing but was stymied by impenetrable fog as he reached France. He downed the plane in a rainy field and awaited rescue under a wing. To his rescuing officer, he offered his apologies: "Monsieur, the plane is intact. I apologize for not having fully completed my first mail flight. I did my best."[6]

The following year, flying as copilot on a mail run from Agadir to Dakar, Saint-Exupéry's Breguet would crash into the dunes on the northern Saharan coast. This event was warmly described many times in Saint-Exupéry's correspondence and published work. René Riguelle was piloting the plane on this leg of the flight, and due to the heat rising from the desert sands decided to take the craft a mile or so off-shore for cooler air. Saint-Exupéry awoke from a nap and, noting the sea below, disapproved. If something went wrong with the plane, he mused, they would drown. Saint-Exupéry resumed his nap. Then there was a jolt, which Riguelle identified as a broken connecting rod. The plane would have to come down. Saint-Exupéry reported a "savage sense of satisfaction" in having known better:

> But this gratifying sense of superiority could obviously not last very long. Riguelle sent the plane earthward in a long diagonal line that brought us within sixty feet of the sand—an altitude at which there was no question of picking out a landing place. We lost both wheels against one sand dune, a wing against another, and crashed with a sudden jerk into a third.
>
> "You hurt?" Riguelle called out.
>
> "Not a bit," I said
>
> "That's what I call piloting a ship," he boasted cheerfully.[7]

The plane had hit the sand at seventy miles an hour and was unfly-able. Saint-Exupéry crawled out on hands and knees, aching all over but substantially unhurt. Shortly after, another mail pilot who had been following them for safety's sake landed nearby in the sand, and a plan was made to take Riguelle and the mail on to Dakar. Since there was no room in the plane for all of them and the mail, Saint-Exupéry was designated to stay behind in the dunes and await pick up on the return flight the next day. There were a few tins of food but no water except for that left in the downed plane's radiator. Because there was a real fear of capture and death at the hands of Saharan Moors, the departing pilots gave their ammunition clips to Saint-Exupéry as a precaution, should he need to use his revolver. His instructions were to shoot at anything he saw.

As it happened, his night alone in the desert was transformative for Saint-Exupéry: "Sitting on the dune, I laid beside me my gun and my cartridge clips. For the first time since I was born it seemed to me that my life was my own and I was responsible for it." Saint-Exupéry was transported by the profound solitude. He looked out over the sea, and at one point a gazelle appeared in the golden light. When his rescuers showed up, he was asked if he had been frightened. He said no, musing that a gazelle was not frightening. Describing the journey to his mother in a letter, he wrote: "the trip went well, apart from a breakdown and the plane crashing in the desert."[8]

Saint-Exupéry would become a seasoned veteran of the North African Aeropostale, claiming to know every dune along the Saharan route. A few years later the firm would transfer him to Buenos Aires, where his deliveries between that city and the southern outposts of Patagonia provided even more exotic adventures. Winds of ninety miles per hour were common, and gale force winds out of the Andes could reach a hundred twenty-five miles per hour—the top speed of the Latécoère 25, the plane Saint-Exupéry and his fellow pilots were given to fly. Saint-Exupéry liked to recount stories of flying at a virtual standstill in the face of such winds. Such conditions once prevented him from reaching a coastal destination to which he had come within six hundred feet. On another flight not long afterward he encountered such a forceful blast that his plane stopped still in midair and began to drop to the earth. When he had fallen to two hundred feet, a blast of air suddenly swept him fifteen hundred feet upward and then five miles out to sea. Helpless to navigate the plane and ferociously battered in his open cockpit, he held on for dear life, hoping his hands could continue to grip the controls and that the plane would not break apart. As the turbulence caused the engine to sputter, the fabric seams of the wings came unglued, and the storage batteries shook loose and flew up through the roof of the plane. His lone passenger, a journalist, attempted to jump out of the cockpit. For an excruciating hour, he managed to regain the five miles back to shore. Only then, sheltered by the coast, did he succeed in reaching his destination, the Patagonian outpost of Comodoro Rivadavia. It took an hour to land the plane, a procedure that involved a ground crew of fourteen, bearing bamboo poles that hooked into eyelets sunk into the bottom of the wings. To counter the wind's force, these landings were made at full throttle. Stabilizing the plane was arduous, dangerous, and occasionally fatal to members of the landing crew. Utterly spent after the seemingly impossible landing, Saint-Exupéry was, at least for the moment, beyond words: "I climbed out of the cockpit and walked off—there was nothing to say."

Whenever possible, Saint-Exupéry liked to lighten the terror of his flying mishaps with incongruous touches. In 1930, flying a circuit to Asunción from Buenos Aires, he offered to take a troop of nine visiting actors and actresses along. The northern leg of the trip went as scheduled but when Saint-Exupéry's plane failed to arrive home on the expected day, a search party was dispatched. Nothing was found. On the afternoon of the second day, Saint-Exupéry's Latécoère came in for a landing at the Buenos Aires airfield. The pilot emerged from the plane unshaven, shoes and trousers covered with mud—and in high spirits. Then his passengers made their way out of the plane, dressed in brightly colored pajamas and bathrobes. As it happened, a terrible storm downed the plane in a muddy expanse of countryside. They opted to slog through the mud until they found a rustic hotel where they were able to purchase only nightclothes. They managed also to buy some parrots, which perched on the actresses' heads as they disembarked. For this, Saint-Exupéry was chastened by a superior for "playing the fool."[9]

Yet, for all his insouciance and eccentricity, Saint-Exupéry was anything but a fool in the way he carried out his responsibilities. His Buenos Aires assignment was in fact a promotion. He was responsible not only for piloting a considerable number of flights himself but also, in his official post as Inspector, for supervising, evaluating, and disciplining his fellow flyers. As his biographer Stacey Schiff put it, "As an administrator Saint-Exupéry was a stickler for discipline if not the rules." Of Saint-Exupéry's work in Argentina, a fellow flyer and friend wrote:

> The Argentines are crazy about him . . . the mail goes through despite the winds, and—despite his absent-minded demeanor—our friend manages the Aeropost Argentina with a firm hand. He flies all day, delivers the mails, lands suddenly 600 miles from Buenos Aires in an airfield whose chief—thinking himself far outside of anyone's purview—is tending to his bridge game and not to his field. Saint-Exupéry rights the situation, takes off again, returns to Pachecho as night falls, picks up his car, races home at full speed, and spends the rest of the night writing. I wonder when he sleeps, this phenomenon![10]

Quite simply, if improbably, Saint-Exupéry was good at his work. Far from debilitating him, his unworldliness served the practical mission of the Aeropostale admirably. By making successful mail delivery a mystical abstraction—the kind of imperative he could understand and embrace—Saint-Exupéry was able to give himself wholly unto its service. "The mail," he had written while learning his trade in North Africa, "is sacred. What is inside has little importance."[11]

But he would continue to crash. Returned to France in 1933, he was employed briefly as a test pilot. One winter afternoon his assignment was to fly and land a seaplane in the frigid waters of the Bay of Saint-Raphaël. Since the pontoons of this craft were angled upward to facilitate takeoff from the water, it was essential in landing to raise the nose of the plane. This was the opposite procedure for landing on a runway, and Saint-Exupéry hit the water nose down, shattering one of the pontoons and pitching the plane violently upside down. One crew member was ejected out into the water, and two others were rescued by a patrol boat, but Saint-Exupéry was trapped inside, immersed in dark, freezing seawater. He groped for the escape hatch in what, he hoped, was the ceiling, but because the plane had flipped over, was actually the floor. When he could no longer hold his breath, he began to breathe in seawater and, he would write later with fascination, to die: "In truth death isn't nearly as disagreeable as they say."[12] He bobbed about for several minutes in this serene and nearly fatal condition. In one account told later, he ran a comb through his hair while under water. Then by chance his head emerged in an air pocket in the tail of the plane, and he began sputtering the bilge out of his lungs. A moment later rescuers pulled him out of the plane and he continued to cough up the swallowed brine. Later he would contrast the peaceful, welcoming approach of death to the jarring discomfort of returning to life.

Two years later, in the course of promoting commercial flight for Air France, Saint-Exupéry found himself piloting another floatplane in Indochina. While ferrying some comrades from Saigon to the Cambodian temples of Angkor, the engine failed twice. The first time Saint-Exupéry was able to land expertly on the Mekong River. When the mechanic succeeded in reviving the engine, the party was briefly airborne again before conking out over the swampy juncture of the Vaico and Soirap Rivers, sixty miles north of Saigon. While the other marooned passengers bunked down warily in the cockpit of the plane—the malarial swamp was infested with snakes and spiders—to await rescue in the morning, Saint-Exupéry was elated by the exotic surroundings. Stretching out over the upper wing, he let loose a barrage of favorite stories, followed by a serenade of old French folk songs. He was resolutely unapologetic when it was learned that the cause of the plane's "failure" was Saint-Exupéry's; he had neglected to fill the gas tanks.

Saint-Exupéry's most famous crash, the one that elevated his celebrity to that of Lindbergh, occurred in 1935 while attempting the world's fastest flight between Paris and Saigon. The Simoun aircraft he would fly had a bigger engine and was faster than the prior record holder's, and Saint-Exupéry was familiar with the route. His preparations, however, were slapdash by any standards. Unlike other celebrated long-distance flyers, he made no training flights in preparation. Unwisely, he opted to fly without a radio in favor of additional fuel storage. And while such ventures typically require a fitness regimen and a period of rest prior to takeoff, Saint-Exupéry made no change in his manic all-night bistro-hopping routine. Indeed in the two days prior to departure, Saint-Exupéry spent much of his time searching nightclubs in pursuit of his wife Consuelo, who had somehow disappeared. One indication of his readiness for the flight was that on the way to the airfield in the small hours of the morning, he found it necessary to make two detours, one to a drugstore to buy a thermos, another to a bistro for coffee to fill it for the flight.

Normally jauntily carefree in the face of a grueling challenge, Saint-Exupéry consulted a fortune-teller the day before his departure. The fortune-teller predicted disaster.

Saint-Exupéry and his friend Prévot, who would accompany him as mechanic, took off from Paris early in the morning on December 29. About twenty hours later, flying blind in heavy winds over the Sahara, Saint-Exupéry sensed he may have overflown Cairo and began a descent. In fact he was more than a hundred miles west of Cairo and was proceeding eastward over the Libyan Desert. Only a radio could have corrected the plane's position. The plane crashed into a sand dune at a speed of 170 miles per hour. Upon impact provisions were thrown 150 feet from the plane. Fearing an explosion, both he and Prévot hurled themselves out of the cockpit. Bruised and shaken up, they were without serious injury. Apart from knowing they were in a remote desert, the two men were lost. Their provisions consisted of the thermos of coffee, some chocolate, and a few crackers.

In the morning, after inscribing the direction they were walking and an SOS onto the fuselage of the Simoun, they set off in a northerly direction. Believing he was in the Sinai desert, Saint-Exupéry knew that he must bear westward to reach Cairo, yet he was troubled by a "vague foreboding."[13] Somehow he could only make his steps go to the east.

As the Parisian press and then the press of other world capitals became aware of the missing airmen, Saint-Exupéry and Prévot hobbled unsteadily through the arid heat for three days. Badly dehydrated, their tongues swollen, and increasingly hallucinatory, they sighted several rescue planes overhead but were unable to make themselves visible to them. On the fourth day in the desert, they encountered a Bedouin mounted on a camel and leading a caravan. The two were offered water and were soon after restored to the safe household of a French couple who would help them get to Cairo. When the news of their survival reached the Hotel Port-Royal in Paris, where an increasingly gloomy vigil had been kept by Saint-Exupéry's wife, his mother, and many friends, the jubilation could not be contained. Saint-Exupéry was celebrated rapturously as a genius of survival, the ultimate romantic hero, a darer, a quester, a life force.

While Saint-Exupéry and Prévot were recovering in the home of the French couple at the desert outpost of Wadi Natroun, the head of the household, a director of the Egyptian Salt and Soda Company, entered his parlor to find two stubbled and tattered Frenchmen smoking cigarettes. Saint-Exupéry was telling his hostess that, "when you have nothing left to hope for, it is easy to die." At which point her husband proposed that some tea and refreshments be provided. "And whiskey," Saint-Exupéry added. "We suffered such terrible thirst in the desert."

Two years later, Saint-Exupéry would suffer a far more serious though less publicized crash. This one nearly killed him. Having arranged a goodwill flight to promote Pan American Airlines, Saint-Exupéry scheduled a 9,000-mile journey from Washington, D.C., to South America. Refueling in Guatemala City en route to Nicaragua, he and Prévot, who had once again signed on as his mechanic, made a careless error. They had their Simoun filled with Imperial instead of American gallons, which rendered the plane too heavy to be airborne after a long taxi down the runway. Saint-Exupéry attempted to lift the plane at the runway's end but could manage no more than seven feet before the Simoun bounced back to earth, sheering its wing on a restraining fence post, then crashing nose first into a gravel pit. The plane was utterly wrecked, and this time the pilots were unable to leap from the wreckage. Prévot was pinned beneath the engine, his leg shattered in several places. Saint-Exupéry was strapped immobile and bloodied in the cockpit. He suffered serious head injuries and multiple fractures, some of which were undiagnosed and partially crippled him for the rest of his life. For days he passed in and out of consciousness in the Guatemala hospital where he stayed for a month. One arm was so badly abraded and infected it would have been amputated but for the special pleading of the patient and his wife, Consuelo, who came to pay her respects. Saint-Exupéry would recover, but he would never afterward be able to lift his arms over his head or bend over to tie his shoes. When, improbably, he was permitted to fly for the French air force in the final years of the Second World War, he required assistance to be suited up in his flight gear, and the pain of doing so was expressed in bitter, ungenerous complaint to those assigned to assist. The Guatemalan crash was the only one of which Saint-Exupéry seems to have been genuinely ashamed. It was the only crash that would not be re-created in his literary work.

Saint-Exupéry never returned from his last flying mission. In July of 1944, he was stationed with his French air unit in Corsica, and though he had already completed the number of missions granted him, he was able to exert the necessary pressure to stay active. To friends and lovers in the States and Europe he had intimated his willingness, even his impatience, to die. The day before his final mission, he wrote a letter to a beloved mistress expressing his "breathtaking indifference to life." A week earlier he had written his wife that his only regret were he shot down would be that it would make her cry.

Saint-Exupéry's assigned mission was to do some mapping reconnaissance over Lyon. Some reports indicate that on the return flight over the Mediterranean Saint-Exupéry's Lightning P-38 was engaged and shot down by a Luftwaffe pilot. Whatever the case, no trace of

Saint-Exupéry or his plane was ever recovered. Years earlier, after the water crash in the bay of Saint-Raphaël, a journalist had asked him what kind of death he preferred. Specifying that his answer was not to be reported until he was actually dead, Saint-Exupéry opined that death by water would be best: "You don't feel yourself dying. You feel simply as if you're falling asleep and beginning to dream."[14]

Earlier it was proposed that Saint-Exupéry's life was shaped by three strong, interrelated impulses: to tell stories, to find those stories in the drama of flight, and to tell the stories to women who would adore him. In the course of his foreshortened life, he would have many romantic lovers and even more dalliances. Women, if they could bear him at all, found him enchanting, often irresistibly so. He was capable of shyness, which rendered him almost mute, but he could also project the winning spontaneity of a precocious child. The women of his heart were very much of a type: ethereal, delicate, utterly impractical, charmed more by image and story than by worldly manifestations.

His first great love was his distant cousin Louise—"Loulou"—de Vilmorin, the youngest daughter of an old aristocratic family, although one more comfortably well off than the Saint-Exupérys. Antoine was twenty-two and Loulou seventeen when they met. Saint-Exupéry was doing a little odd job flying in Paris but was still chiefly supported by an allowance from his mother. Louise was then and would all her life remain an exotic figure. When Saint-Exupéry met her, she was lying fetchingly in her bed, to which she was more or less confined for three years due to a hip ailment. Her chamber was accessible by its own staircase on the top floor of the de Vilmorins' eccentric Parisian house, and it was a popular destination for suitors, friends, and her brothers and sisters. One admirer described Loulou's situation at the time.

> At the very top of the de Vilmorin's townhouse, in a room which was
> a roost, an exquisite room, admirably appointed, there was in a bed,

the most exquisite creature imaginable, the quintessential young lady, in a light pink nightshirt, smoking Craven A's; she was poetry itself, poetry incarnate, charm incarnate; the small face of this creature was something from a dream, a waking dream, it was a marvelous vision further enhanced by an entirely irresistible chirping. She was highly intelligent, entirely precious, she was absolutely stunning.[15]

Loulou was quickly taken with her kindred spirit cousin, and he fell madly in love with her, but he would have to contend with many others for her affection. Loulou's circle formed a mock society, the GB Club, dedicated to fostering "the growth of healthy ribaldry." The bylaws encouraged bawdiness, brawling, tasteless humor, and forbade any discussion of politics and religion. The club adopted a color, a mascot, a favored brand of cigarettes, and preferred wines. Saint-Exupéry's name appeared at the bottom of the list of officers. His title was Grand Poéte Sentimental et Comique.

Like Saint-Exupéry, Loulou was steeped in literature and poetry—but in her case there was nothing else, no science, mathematics, or history. She played the cello, painted, and recited poetry at length. A typical story of hers began: "There was once a man who married a huge bureau, in each drawer of which was a child."[16] It is hard to imagine a young woman more immediately appealing to Saint-Exupéry. Nor were his charms altogether lost on her. Many years later she would recall him as "the magician of our adolescence. A minstrel, a knight, a noble magus, a child of mystery, full of grace."

Moreover, Loulou would be a true heiress, and the Saint-Exupérys were at best shabby genteel. When Saint-Exupéry announced to his mother in 1923 that he and Louise were engaged, Madame Saint-Exupéry thoroughly approved and sent the bride-to-be a set of family heirloom pearls. The pearls were appraised critically by Louise who sent them out to be restrung. The de Vilmorins were not enthusiastic about the proposed match. An aviator husband might be a bad bet on many counts. Saint-Exupéry at that time held no real job and was otherwise without means. Moreover his appeal could be elusive; it was not impossible to view him as oafish and merely odd. It was Loulou's brothers who labeled him "the vague pachyderm."

After a heady but brief period of engagement, Loulou began to have doubts. A precipitating cause was Saint-Exupéry's 1923 crash in the Hanriot HP14, which battered him to the extent he required hospital treatment and an extended cure afterward at Vichy. Loulou sent a sister to Saint-Exupéry in the hospital to tell him that her sister could not possibly be married to a man susceptible to such accidents. Deeply in love, Saint-Exupéry promised to give up flying.

Though they would experience intermittent bouts of happiness, as when Saint-Exupéry would tell his flying tales—"he describes for me terrifying or sublime moments spent between the sky and the earth"— Loulou would ultimately break off the engagement. Saint-Exupéry had not succeeded in finding a position, and his accrued debts stemming from the crash were unpaid. Slow to return to health, he had himself examined for syphilis, as he would often do later in his life, but his worries on that score proved groundless.

Saint-Exupéry would never entirely get over Loulou de Vilmorin. She was something of a romantic obsession even after his marriage in 1931. He would dedicate to her his first book, *Night Flight,* and the manuscript of his second. Shortly after their breakup, Loulou married a wealthy American entrepreneur sixteen years older than she. The next time Saint-Exupéry laid eyes on her—a fleeting recognition as she was exiting a cab—she was pregnant. He would continue to write her love letters.

Like Saint-Exupéry, Loulou would never succeed at domestic life nor would she be capable of remaining faithful to a romantic partner. She would go on to publish fourteen novels and three collections of poems. She once stated to a companion, "I shall love you forever, tonight." On another occasion she observed, "I have no faith in my fidelity." She would die at sixty-nine, but even in her sixties an admirer noted that she remained "attached to the magic of her childhood."[17]

Although Saint-Exupéry was quixotically devoted to his wife,

Consuelo, until he died, he seemed always to require the stimulation and comfort of other women. In contrast to Consuelo, who was a dark and delicate Latin sylph, the "other women" were typically lithe, leggy blondes, intelligent, literary, preferably aristocratic, and strikingly beautiful. One of them, who took pains to keep their relationship out of official, public view, served as a kind of counter-wife. Designated by Saint-Exupéry's principal biographer only as "Madame de B, although widely known to be the Parisian socialite Nelly de Vogüe," she was married and comfortably wealthy when she met the promising young writer-aviator in 1929. Charmed by both the man and his work, her first overture to him was to send him a check when she learned he was in financial difficulties. That check would not be cashed, although Saint-Exupéry, in even more desperate circumstances, would accept her assistance later. Known in Parisian social and literary circles as "la blonde," she would read Saint-Exupéry's manuscript, advising and encouraging him. To her, he would confide his practical and domestic troubles. She seems to have been selfless and endlessly accommodating of his quirks and needs. Stacy Schiff recounts an episode when Saint-Exupéry was badly broke and learned that Consuelo had had yet another auto accident, in Dijon, and needed immediate attention. Madame de B purchased tickets for them both and providing a picnic lunch, she escorted Saint-Exupéry on the train ride to Dijon where, on arrival, he went off to find Consuelo, and she changed platforms for the return trip. It was on this excursion that she realized she wished she were not married to another. Saint-Exupéry and Madame de B's privileged relationship was well known to Consuelo, and it was a source of aggravated domestic storms, but the pair continued to commune. When Saint-Exupéry hovered near death after crashing on the Guatemala airstrip, he instructed that Madame de B be informed that he had survived—and then he lost consciousness. On the eve of his disappearance in 1944, the last letter he wrote was to Madame de B. It was speculated by one biographer that she provided both the "space" and the "grounding" he needed to go on living.[18]

After the collapse of the French fighting forces in 1940, Saint-Exupéry made his way to New York where, until he returned to active service, he became romantically involved with a succession of beautiful women. To one of them, Natalie Paley, a Romanov princess and actress, he professed his love, he claimed, for the last time. To another, Silvia Reinhardt, he would recount his innermost troubles when he visited her unannounced in the small hours. Her French was spotty and his English almost nonexistent, and as he read to her from his manuscripts-in-progress, she would listen appreciatively, moved to tears, not understanding a word. Silvia Reinhardt would provide him the doll with its blond corona of curls, which, propped on the arm of the sofa where he wrote and sketched in her Park Avenue apartment, became the model for the Little Prince.

Saint-Exupéry detested coarseness and sexual vulgarity and, with a reflexive aristocratic discretion, did not boast of his conquests. Although Consuelo would follow him to New York, they set up in separate residences, occasionally socializing as a couple, nearly always squabbling. His own philandering did not prevent him from being intensely jealous of Consuelo, who took pains to establish herself as a *femme fatale*. Returning from Silvia's flat in the early morning hours, he would call in at Consuelo's, only to learn that she had not yet returned home.

Saint-Exupéry's later affairs were not primarily sexual, if they were sexual at all. He was generally in poorish health, suffering from gall bladder inflammations and headaches in addition to the skeletal injuries resulting from his crashes. Although there is ample female testimony from that period as to his charismatic aura in public and to his sex appeal—including a rapturous account by the actress Fay Wray—he seems to have had trouble performing sexually. Consuelo confused and intrigued her New York intimates by confiding, alternately, that her husband had just had his way with her and that he was no longer capable of relations due to so much high altitude flying. By all accounts, too, Saint-Exupéry was a very heavy drinker, particularly in the evening, which cannot have helped his performance. What he required was rapt attention from beautiful and admiring women, women who would listen to his stories. Several of them would attest that their assignations with Saint-Exupéry were like no other kind of experience: elevated, intense, soulful, not really of this world.

It is not surprising that Saint-Exupéry, however difficult he found it to live with her, would meet his soul mate in the strange and diminutive figure of Consuelo. Consuelo Suncin Sandoval was born on a coffee plantation in El Salvador. She was named Consuelo—"consolation"—to commemorate the bereavement her parents felt at the loss of her four brothers who had died in their infancy before she was born. Astonishingly vital herself, she would survive all three of her husbands, including Saint-Exupéry. A product of Spanish and Mayan ancestors, she was dark, delicate, and tiny. Verifying even essential details of her life is nearly impossible as she was an inspired fabricator. In these fabrications Saint-Exupéry seems to have found what he most longed for: a woman who was sheer story.

As such she is a remarkable story. Born in 1901 in the Salvadoran countryside (although she would later revise her birth date to 1907), she felt as a child that she was destined to be a princess. She liked to tell the story of how as a little girl she had shed her clothes, smeared her body with honey, and cavorted through the rain forest until, covered with living, fluttering butterflies, she wore the most beautiful dress in the world. In a variant of the story, she was born nearly dead, and a sorcerer covered her body with honey to attract bees whose stings roused her to life. The credibility of such tales mattered less to the friends and lovers she captivated than did the compelling and melodious telling.

There was a distinct *la belle dame sans merci* quality to Consuelo, which in reality made her—literally—hard to live with. When, as an arrestingly exotic young beauty, she met Saint-Exupéry in Buenos Aires, she was already twice widowed. Her first husband, a young Mexican army officer died suddenly of an illness within a year of their wedding. For three years she was mistress to the Mexican philosopher-statesman, José Vasconcelos, who wrote of her: "to hear her tell a story was to fall under a spell." Vasconcelos would introduce her to Parisian society, where she won the heart of the writer-statesman Enrique Gómez Carillo. Carillo was more than thirty years her senior, but there was about him, too, a romantic, fantastic aura; he was a former consort of Isadora Duncan and was rumored to have arranged the entrapment of Mata Hari. As Senora Carillo, Consuelo was temporarily well off until, after only a year, Carillo suffered a sudden stroke and died.

Consuelo's account of her initial encounter with Saint-Exupéry would strain all credulity, were it not for the young flyer's well-documented eccentricity. She had been invited to visit Argentina by some associates of her late husband, and at a cocktail reception found herself in the presence of a towering, unshaven Frenchman who arrived, late, fresh from two days of mail flights. "The dark-haired man was so tall," she wrote in a posthumously published memoir, "I had to raise my eyes to the sky in order to see him." Informed that Saint-Exupéry was a distinguished aviator, she announced, "I don't like to fly. I don't like things that go fast. I don't like seeing too many faces at once. And I want to leave."

Saint-Exupéry, she reported, would have none of it. Physically forcing her down into a chair next to him, he told her: "But you know very well you're coming with me in my plane to see the Rio de la Plata from beyond the clouds. It's fantastically beautiful, and you'll see a sunset like none other in the world." When Consuelo said that this would be impossible because, in addition to her aversion to flying, she was meeting friends, Saint-Exupéry informed her that her friends must join them. At that point, the flyer excused himself to telephone her party to invite them on the twilight excursion and, after stopping at a barber's to shave, bundled Consuelo into his car to take her to the airstrip. A bus was sent for her friends. En route Saint-Exupéry told her of his experiences flying at night. She told him he should really write them down, to which he responded that he had already written a book, *Southern Mail*: "I'll give you a copy. It was a complete flop. I sold three copies, one to my aunt, another to my sister, and another to a friend of my sister's. . . . People laughed at me, but if you say my stories are good, I'll write them down. I'll do it for you alone, a very long letter."

Boarding the plane, the friends were directed to the passenger seats, Consuelo to a seat in the cockpit next to him, separated from the cabin by a curtain. She noted his hands on the controls: "beautiful, intelligent, wiry hands, both delicate and strong." As soon as they were airborne, one of the beautiful hands found her knee, and Saint-Exupéry said, "Will you kiss me?" Responding that she was newly widowed and in the habit of kissing only people she loved, Saint-Exupéry would not be deterred.

"Kiss me or I'll drown you," he said, making as if to plunge the plane into the ocean.

I bit on my handkerchief. Why did I have to kiss a man I'd only just met? . . .

"Is this how you persuade women to kiss you?"

. . . Then he gazed at me, cut off the power, and said, "I know what it is. You won't kiss me because I'm ugly."

I saw tears like pearls rolling from his eyes down onto his necktie, and my heart melted with tenderness. I leaned over as best I could and kissed him. He kissed me back violently, and we stayed like that for two or three minutes while the plane rose and fell as he cut the power off and revved it back up again. All the passengers were sick. . . .

"No, you're not ugly," I said, "but you're too strong for me. You're hurting me. You don't kiss me, you bite me, you eat me. I want to land now."

"Forgive me," he said. "I don't know much about women. I love you because you're a child and you're scared."

"You're going to hurt me in the end. You're quite mad."

"I only seem to be. I always do whatever I want, even when it's bad for me."[19]

In the days that followed, as Buenos Aires erupted in a violent revolution, Consuelo realized she was in love with the ardent and impetuous airman. Puzzled and at times even appalled by his unpredictability, she felt powerfully drawn to him. He would absent himself for days at a time delivering the Patagonian mails, then appear suddenly at her hotel ready to go dancing.

> Once, arriving at my hotel and watching me drink a glass of water, he said, "Oh! I know what I need. I haven't had a drink since yesterday. Pour me a drink."
>
> I handed him a glass of water and a bottle of cognac. He poured the whole bottle of cognac down his throat and then the water, without thinking. He had forgotten that the other people who were there might also want a drink. He didn't bother to excuse himself for this because he hated to lose the thread of his conversation. That really irritated him. If he was interrupted during one of his stories, he would sometimes remain silent for the rest of the evening. Or I should say for the whole night, since he never had any notion what time it was. . . .
>
> . . . Tireless as he was, he could be annoyed at having to make the simplest gestures. For example, he hated to go to the trouble of tapping the ashes from his cigarette into an ashtray. Even if they were dropping into the folds of his pants, he would ignore them to keep from interrupting a conversation, seemingly oblivious to the state of his clothing. So what if his pants caught fire![20]

Saint-Exupéry often noted that Consuelo looked sad, and he found this very appealing. She told him: "I look sad because I don't have the courage to escape from you . . . for you, I am nothing but a dream."

Consuelo may have been shrewd in acknowledging that she was more a dream to her beloved than a flesh-and-blood woman, but she would be a persistently recurring dream. He would take her back with him to France where they would marry—Consuelo still in widow's black. They would never settle peacefully in a residence. Saint-Exupéry's writing and flying assignments, financial embarrassments, and finally the war dislocated the couple from Nice to Paris to Casablanca to New York. They suffered their most strained relations in Paris when Saint-Exupéry was not flying. His mounting literary reputation bore no relation to his modest income, which in any case he overspent at cafes, where he would not only eat and drink without regard to cost but, whenever in funds, pick up the check for all those gathered at his table. He was invited out nightly, and his company included titled aristocrats, literary eminences, demimonde bohemians, and exotic decadents. Unable to break his habit of all-night carousing, he would tell Consuelo his parties were a chore for him, and it would not really be seemly for his wife to join him—but he invited her to call him, to provide an excuse, rarely actually offered, for an early departure. When on occasion Consuelo did appear at an evening outing, she was hurt and undone by "the pretty blond heads" fawning over her exuberant husband as he held forth, telling his stories of flight, performing his spectacular card tricks.

> He came home with his handkerchiefs covered in lipstick; I didn't want to be jealous, but it was starting to depress me. People would tell me, "We ran into Tonio in a car with two women." "Yes," he explained, "Two secretaries from *The New French Review* who invited me to stop off and have some port at their place on the way home."[21]

Consuelo would claim to have learned to "swallow the venom of jealousy," but she also increasingly indulged her own romantic inclinations. For years afterward, she would summon up feelings ranging from abandonment to outrage that her husband could so blatantly seek his pleasures elsewhere.

> A woman friend of yours was sitting on the floor at your feet with her guitar, singing very beautiful melodies. She even let her hair down and was leaning her head between your legs with funny

little jerking movements: it all made a delightful erotic tableau. I was too young; I wasn't used to the lax ways of Parisian artistic circles—the "high life"—and you told me, "Go back home, *ma petite fille*. I know you're shocked by certain types of behavior, but they're entirely natural. It's just that I need my freedom."[22]

She writes of taking a dashing new lover, a poet named Andre, and summoning the courage to tell Saint-Exupéry that she had fallen in love and was, sadly, leaving him. Saint-Exupéry implored her not to, but when she insisted, he told her then to call for Andre to come take her away. When she did so and Andre arrived at the door, Saint-Exupéry greeted him—for some reason bare-chested—and offered drinks all around. "Tonio looked very strong with his hairy chest," Consuelo wrote, "and he was very cheerful." They drank Pernod for a while, and Andre departed the scene.

Just as often, however, Saint-Exupéry was not on hand to interfere with his wife's romantic distractions, and on one occasion he offered money to a lover if he would take her out to dine, as he was exhausted from flying and wanted to sleep. On one especially bizarre occasion before Saint-Exupéry departed for New York, he and Consuelo were living separately, he in a flat in Paris, she in a rustic house in the country. In the course of visiting the country house, Saint-Exupéry was so demonstrably taken with Consuelo's pretty young maid, Vera—and Vera with him—that Consuelo confessed sympathy for the girl who, like so many, had fallen under her husband's spell. As suspected, Vera was thereafter wildly infatuated with Saint-Exupéry. Not long afterward, hearing that he was ill, Consuelo decided to visit her husband unannounced in his flat. Vera begged to go, having prepared some treats for the ailing patient, and Consuelo assented. When they gained entry into Saint-Exupéry's rooms, it was clear that he was not alone. A shiny green skirt was seen to flit into the lavatory where it continued to flash and rustle, while from the bedroom Saint-Exupéry shouted that his visitors were uninvited, unwelcome, and that they should leave at once. Consuelo persisted.

"I'm worried about you," I said calmly. "Nothing else matters . . ."

"I've never treated you like this before," he said miserably. "Shouting to chase you away . . ."

Both of us were weeping, and Vera was sobbing as she watched.

"You are a monster," [Vera] cried. "If you knew the trouble I went to make this bouquet . . ."

I pushed her out the door. I believe Vera finally understood that just being pretty isn't enough for a woman to become and remain part of a man's life.[23]

In all the tragicomic betrayals, partings, and tender reunions that would follow, Consuelo would indeed remain a part of Saint-Exupéry's life. Later, living their adjacent existences in New York, he would pace frantically outside her apartment at three in the morning, so agitated by her absence that he would write her long letters protesting her heartless cruelty to one who loved and needed her so much. At such moments he could also confess:

You were painfully bruised by the struggles of our daily life. Your impatience grew out of your weariness, and mine as well. Worry took the place of love, and I left you in order to protect us from each other. Our friends have been wrong to hold you responsible for my happiness or unhappiness. You must know that I have never stopped loving you.[24]

Saint-Exupéry's last letter to Consuelo, composed just a week before he disappeared, concluded:

Thank you for being my wife. If I am wounded, I will have someone to take care of me, if I am killed, I will have someone to wait for in eternity, and if I come back, I will have someone to come back to.[25]

The year before his disappearance, Saint-Exupéry published his strange and stirring book for children, *The Little Prince*. The story begins whimsically and ends in a sad, almost unbearable evocation of loss and longing. The tale is narrated by an unnamed flyer who, six years prior to the telling, crashed a plane in the Sahara. The narrative spans the eight days the flyer's plane was downed.

Saint-Exupéry clearly intended to write this story for children, or at least the spirit of children. The book is dedicated to his beloved friend, Leon Werth—with an "apology" to children for dedicating the story to a "grown-up." In the course of excusing himself, Saint-Exupéry actually amends the dedication from "To Leon Werth" to "To Leon Werth When He Was a Little Boy."

The flyer-narrator begins with a brief discourse on the limitations of grown-ups in understanding children and in understanding the world generally. He reveals that at age six he was an aspiring artist, but his inspiration was squelched by grown-ups who could not see the inner truth in his work. Specifically, the grown-ups could not see what was represented in his drawing of a boa constrictor that had swallowed an elephant. They thought it was a hat—because it looked like a hat.

> I showed the grown-ups my masterpiece, and I asked them if my drawing scared them.
> They answered, "Why be scared of a hat?"[26]

Having decided, at six, that his art was futile, the narrator remarks, "Grown-ups never understand anything by themselves, and it is exhausting for children to have to provide explanations over and over again."

The narrator loses not only his imaginative art at six, he loses all genuine and soulful contact with others: "So I lived all alone, without anyone I could really talk to, until I had to make a crash landing in the Sahara Desert six years ago." Six years prior to composing *The Little Prince*, Saint-Exupéry had crashed, with Prévot, in the Libyan Desert. He might also have been recalling his solitary night in the dunes when he was left with only his revolver and cartridge clips—the night he first realized "my life was completely my own."

It is in such abandoned solitude that the narrator encounters the Little Prince in the desert at nightfall. The Little Prince happens also to be six, and he is—or was—the sole inhabitant of a tiny asteroid, Asteroid B-612, unobservably far off in the heavens. The Little Prince speaks in the voice and in the logic of the narrator when he was six. With a beguiling indirection the Little Prince tells the flyer he has, via a harnessed flock of birds, departed Asteroid B-612 to solve a desperate problem, a problem of the heart. The Little Prince knows without being told the flyer's innermost nature and that he is a suppressed artist. Moreover, the Little Prince wants the flyer to draw him a sheep.

The Little Prince asks the flyer to draw him a sheep because he needs one to help him tend his planet. More particularly, he needs a sheep to eat the sprouts of baobab trees that threaten to overgrow and destroy Asteroid B-612. But while a sheep might help to preserve the little planet, it could also do a profound harm: it might eat the solitary rose who is the love of the Little Prince's life. The rose, we learn, is self-absorbed, vain, and petulant, but she, too, has the irresistible spark of childhood—and she loves the Little Prince as he loves her.

So, in effect, the journey to secure a sheep is an adultlike gesture in the direction of practical accommodation. As such, it is inherently problematic and will necessitate the loss of some of the life-giving liberty and spontaneity of the puer spirit. The sheep will keep the baobabs in check, but the rose will be safe only if tended and protected. Doing so will entail commitment, foresight, and work on the Little Prince's part.

In the course of resolving to make this commitment—to protect the beloved rose and thus be "responsible"—the Little Prince recounts to the flyer his experiences traveling from his asteroid to the desert. He visits six eccentric planets before alighting on Earth. Each is occupied by a single person, an adult, and each of these is a distinctive type.

The first planet is inhabited by a King whose existence is driven by the imperative to be in authority and to command compliance. His comic imperiousness cannot hide the more elemental fact of his loneliness, and he cannot persuade the Little Prince to stay even with enticements of office and titles. The next two planets are even less alluring. On one he meets a vain man who craves applause and does not know why. On the other lives a drunkard who is chronically ashamed that he drinks and then drinks to forget his shame.

On the fourth planet the Little Prince encounters a businessman, who stimulates a much stronger, more substantial response from the boy visitor. The businessman can barely be engaged in conversation because he is obsessed with counting things. Grown-ups, the Little Prince had already observed, are so preoccupied with numbers they lose sight altogether of the particular realities the numbers refer to. When the Little Prince asks the businessman why he is counting the stars, the boy is told "so that I can own them." When asked the purpose of owning the stars, the businessman replies that it is to put them down on a slip of paper and to deposit the slip of paper in a bank. The businessman professes repeatedly that his life is "serious," but the Little Prince finds such a life neither serious nor useful.

On the fifth planet, the Little Prince finds a lamplighter who frantically makes his rounds, extinguishing the planet's lone lamp at daybreak, lighting it again at sunset, the lighting and extinguishing following each other almost immediately due to the tininess of the planet. In this instance, the Little Prince's impression of the planet's occupant is thoughtfully unresolved. The Little Prince is touched by the lamplighter's commitment to his duty, but he cannot see—nor can the lamplighter—the source that compels such an admirable commitment.

On the sixth planet the Little Prince meets a geographer who writes massive, authoritative books on his findings. Believing that the geographer must know important and useful information about where things are and what they are like, the Little Prince is disappointed to learn the geographer does not even know the particular features of his own planet. He relies, he says, on *explorers* to gather actual data; it is his far greater responsibility to record it. Again, as with the problem of numbers and their referents, the Little Prince confronts the rift between "knowledge about" and "experience of."

Which brings the Little Prince to Earth. The earth is vastly larger than the other planets he visits, and the Little Prince has a number of formative encounters before he meets the stranded flyer in the desert. The first of these is with a moon-yellow cobra who discourses in riddles. The Little Prince will reckon with him later. For a time the Little Prince wanders the earth, scaling peaks, taking in the vastness of the given world, an experience that makes him very lonely, and he remembers the beautiful sense of connectedness he feels to his beloved rose. But then he confronts an existential puzzle: a garden of five thousand roses. How, he wonders, can his one rose be a true source of inspiration and meaning if it is a mere instance of a common thing, of which there is a boundless plenitude? This troubles the Little Prince whose love for his rose assumed that she was unique, a novelty. There was only one, and she was only his. But here, on this other sphere of existence—earth—there are endless instances of everything and therefore, endless difficulties in determining what, and which ones, to love.

At this point the Little Prince meets a fox, who turns out to be helpful. The fox professes at first not to be much interested in problems of loneliness, love, and relationship. He is interested in stealing and eating peoples' chickens, also in avoiding hunters. But as they converse, the Little Prince and the Fox establish a friendly bond. At one point, the Little Prince confesses that he is lonely and asks the Fox to play with him. The Fox says that would be impossible unless the Little Prince tames him. When the Little Prince asks what "tame" means, the Fox tells him it means "to create ties." Moreover, the fox explains, to create ties opens up a new realm of understanding: "the only things you learn are the things you tame." But there is a corresponding burden to bear: to tame results in needing and being needed.

"People have forgotten the truth," the Fox said, "But you mustn't forget it. You become responsible for what you've tamed. You're responsible for your rose . . ."

"I'm responsible for my rose . . . ," the Little Prince repeated, in order to remember.[27]

The lesson of taming strikes a responsive chord in the Little Prince, and when he revisits the garden of many roses, he realizes that none of them is like his special, beloved rose, because he has tended and cared for her. He has "created ties."

It is the eighth day of the flyer's desolation when the Little Prince finishes his account of these adventures. The plane still has not been repaired, and they have run out of water. Although the flyer is dubious about the suggestion, the Little Prince persuades him to go off together in search of a well. Night falls as they make their way over the sands. Though they are both thirsty and there is little reason to hope, the Little Prince shares an epiphany: a revealed truth even more profound than the meaning of taming. The Little Prince explains to the flyer that the stars are so beautiful and alive because they conceal a flower he can't see. The flyer does not understand this statement. But then, when the Little Prince tells him that the desert is also beautiful because it conceals an unseen mystery—a well—the flyer begins to understand that the truest, most essential realities are always concealed. What makes things beautiful, the Little Prince explains, is always invisible.

In the dead of night the Little Prince falls asleep on the sand. The flyer gathers him up into his arms and walks on. As he does so, he is overcome with feeling for the Little Prince—if not for the little creature he is carrying, at least for the invisible beauty he conceals.

I was moved. It was as if I was carrying a fragile treasure. It actually seemed to me there was nothing more fragile on earth. By the light of the moon, I gazed at that pale forehead, those closed eyes, those locks of hair trembling in the wind, and I said to myself, *what I'm looking at is only a shell. What's most important is invisible.*[28]

At daybreak they find a well and drink. This enables the flyer to complete his plane's repairs and to live. The Little Prince, however, has made an arrangement with the yellow snake whose lethal bite that evening returns him to his little planet and his beloved rose. This is, of course, unendurably sad for the flyer who, after all, has been granted the rarest of gifts: he has confronted his own puer spirit, listened to it, gathered it up, and held it fast to his heart as he walked under the desert stars. He was able to feel again the eternal boy spirit, feel its beauty and affirm it. Moreover, he learned what the boy spirit has to teach a man. Not long before he disappears, the Little Prince tells the flyer that thereafter when he looked up into a starry sky, "You'll have stars like nobody else."

"It's all a great mystery," the flyer concludes. But it's a mystery he now understands as only a child understands:

> As for me, nothing in the universe can be the same if somewhere, no one knows where, a sheep we never saw has or has not eaten a rose . . .
>
> And no grown-up will ever understand how such a thing could be so important![29]

The "great mystery" Saint-Exupéry celebrated in *The Little Prince* is the beautiful and devastating precariousness of puer spirit embodied and felt. To catch a glimpse of it, to experience an ephemeral instant of it, is to be transported to a pitch of ecstasy otherwise indescribable— and to suffer a simultaneous intimation of its loss. The quest for it is the most beautiful quest. To achieve it at all is to awaken the dread of its loss—and then to lose it. This is the mystery, or the drama, of every boy who lives to manhood. However fleetingly, he feels what Icarus felt, then flies where Icarus flew—or is coaxed deadeningly down to "the middle course."

When, as a young pilot in training, Saint-Exupéry was assigned his first mail flight over the Pyrenees, he wrote of waking before dawn and riding an old omnibus to the airstrip. The other passengers are Aeropostale clerks, deskmen. To these "middle course" compromisers Saint-Exupéry offers up a heartfelt condolence.

> Old bureaucrat, my comrade, it is not you who are to blame. No one ever helped you to escape. You, like a termite, built your peace by blocking up with cement every chink and cranny through which the light might pierce. You rolled yourself up into a ball in your genteel security, in routine, in the stifling conventions of provincial life, raising a modest rampart against the winds and tides and the stars. You have chosen not to be disturbed by great problems, having trouble enough to forget your own fate as a man. You are not the dweller on an errant planet and do not ask questions for which there are no answers . . . Nobody grasped you by the shoulder while there was still time. Now the clay of which you are shaped has dried and hardened, and naught in you will ever awaken the sleeping musician, the poet, the astronomer that possibly inhabited you in the beginning.[30]

Saint-Exupéry's highly distinctive life can be seen as a heroic attempt to come to living terms with the puer spirit. He tried fervently and foolishly to live in that spirit, and he made repeated attempts to tell the story of doing so. He told the story to his Consuelo, who was the rose of *The Little Prince,* and to other beloved women he tamed. He wanted, always, to play. When he learned to fly, he could never really hold the middle course—or want to. Saint-Exupéry embodied Icarus in a world held by Daedalus. As a puer-spirited man, he stirred in other men a profound, beckoning disturbance, an un-nameable longing; and he kindled pure desire in the hearts of women.

# 6

## ICARUS OBSERVED FROM THE GROUND

THE SPECTACLE OF two winged figures, Daedalus and Icarus, soaring overhead could only be regarded with amazement by those who saw them.

The first—and every—intimation of the puer spirit alive and aloft in the world releases an ecstatic response. There is an all-being sense of affirmation: *yes, it's true!* Something deeper than good sense and cultural armor rises up to meet the transcendent boy. The witness wholeheartedly and irrationally cheers for him. Such intimations are rare, and they are always a surprise. In the ancient world, as the Homeric era was passing into Hellenic civilization, the transcendent boy, often Dionysus, was a figure in mystery religions, which were then suppressed. Thereafter the puer might surface more safely—and harmlessly, from the civic perspective—in fancy, dreams, and art. Today such intimations are likely to be experienced in the strangely privileged and tightly bounded theater of rock concerts, especially those held by groups with cult followings like the Grateful Dead and Phish. In such settings, the irrational and even the illicit are given a kind of uneasy permission to surface collectively. Intoxication is votive rather than recreational. There is every expectation of boundaries dissolved, of rapt communion, of release. In such a sensory and spiritual climate, the performers need only appear, re-create their familiar trademark sounds in order to catalyze the collective release. The publicity and commercial promotion of the cultic performers can carry the ecstatic promise of the experience out into the larger, civic order—with an impact that is simultaneously exhilarating and disturbing. There are no terms or categories available to the civic sensibility to describe the appeal of the cult figures; there is every term and category to describe the disturbance. The cult figures are necessarily outrageous. They are at once gypsies, vagabonds, sorcerers, criminals. Their physical appearance serves in every age to negate all conventions of appearance. The sixties rock musical *Hair* understood the deep psychological tension between cultural restriction and hair. To grow it to unruly length, to shave it stunningly off, to tease it out into sculpted oddities, to dye it blue or orange or pink are ways of saying yes to the forever unnamable. To undress or to dress across gender expectation, to dress out of historical period, to wear underwear as outerwear, to dress in spangles or feathers or tatters is to approach the same release.

The cult entertainers invite both the release and the disturbance. Dangerously defiant of the civic order and ultimately not assimilable into it, they achieve a sudden, phenomenal celebrity, then disappear, having run finally afoul of the law or standards of decency. Their planes or cars crash, or there is a fatal overdose. Yet, for the duration of the flash of their impact, they are seemingly everywhere—and seemingly everything. Such, for a spell, was Elagabalus, the painted boy emperor of Rome, parading in saffron robes and jewels in his glittering chariot through throngs of ecstatic citizens. Such, too, perhaps, was Michael Jackson, once the most ebullient and cutest of little boys, who would subsequently carve and tint and coif his face and form out of any imaginable human category. As freak-celebrity, Michael Jackson was no-age, no-gender, no civic type. But whatever he was, he was always, somehow, a boy.

The next reaction to the transcendent boy sets in so powerfully and often so soon that it can eclipse any conscious sense or memory of the initial exhilaration. This reaction is sheer disapproval, and it carries with it the force of righteous indignation. The disapproval is communicable; it resonates publicly, for the civic order knows well what is most likely to negate and undo it. There is no longer any permissible wonder that a boy is aloft, soaring toward heaven. Instead there is an unspoken sense of betrayal, of the very deepest standards being violated. Boys do not fly. They do not get high. They should not desire or be allowed to seek ecstasy. If some engineer or chemist creates the material means to fly, such flight must be scheduled and purposeful, maintaining the safe and certain "middle course" Daedalus prescribed for Icarus.

In this way the civic order hardens against the transcendent boy. He has, after all, profaned everything sacred: flags, icons, rituals, creeds. He manages to say or sing precisely the things the civic order cannot bear to hear, to look and behave in ways most certain to shock and anger. Sexually, he promises to be polymorphously promiscuous. The mood he creates crackles with violence. The wild abandon of rock and roll gropes blindly in the direction of terrorism. This rock star likes to set his stage showily ablaze. That one smashes his guitar to splinters. Yet another is cheered for biting off the head of a live bat. The transcendent boy is a bad boy, the worst boy. He can sometimes be arrested and locked up, but he's always out again; he will perish on his own manic schedule.

Because of the transcendent boy's celebrity and his oddity, the civil order occasionally wants to stage a commercial viewing. These are always bizarre affairs. The attempt on the part of the civic order to meet its negation never really comes off. There is always the impression of a slightly cowed and unctuous Ed Sullivan in his funereal black suit, his neck and shoulders seemingly fused in lifelong discomfort—greeting Elvis or Jim Morrison or Mick Jagger. The atmosphere in the studio is so charged with sex and the promise of ecstatic release that it seems near combustion. The quivering girls shriek and squeal through and over Ed Sullivan's faltering greetings, as he calls them "fine boys," "wonderful boys."

They are always boys, not men. This need never be said, but it is deeply felt. Something insistent but inarticulate in each citizen first cries out for and then condemns the transcendent boy. We long for his release, his real presence in the world. Then there is a thrilling intimation. Then the relentless suppression of that intimation. Americans, for instance, might sense the untamable, irrepressible puer spirit in their president. They may, along with the rest of the package, vote that spirit into office. Inevitably, there will follow the unthinkable, nonassimilable behavior or gesture. And then, of course, the Starr Commission sets to work.

From the standpoint of civil order, Starr Commissions always have the last word. This is because the civil order keeps records and thus tells the civic story. Transcendent boys leave barely a trace; the feelings evoked by their ephemeral appearances are, like those attached to dreams, elusive, easy to forget. The more longstanding and outwardly stable the civil order, the more likely it is that the puer spirit will be unacknowledged. Modern consciousness finds ways simply not to see it. Indeed, not seeing it is a necessary precondition for modern civilization.

W. H. Auden deftly captured this habit of normative non-seeing in his poem, "Musée des Beaux Arts," a reflection on how old master painters depict people carrying out their daily lives oblivious to instances of the miraculous occurring in plain sight.

> *In Breuguel's* Icarus, *for instance:*
> *How everything turns away*
> *Quite leisurely from the disaster; the ploughman*
>     *may*
> *Have heard the splash, the forsaken cry,*
> *But for him it was not an important failure; the sun*
>     *shone*
> *As it had to on the white legs disappearing into the*
>     *green*

*Water; and the expensive delicate ship that must have*
  *seen*
*Something amazing, a boy falling out of the sky,*
*Had somewhere to get to and sailed callously on.*[1]

Breughel's painting is, if anything, more aware of the non-seeing than the poem. The viewer is presented with a sweeping panorama of an expanse of sea girded by high promontories of settled farmland. Farmers are busy tilling the fields behind oxen and plough. The eaves and steeples of towns can be seen in the distance. Merchant vessels ply the waters. Only the painting's title—*Icarus*—would alert the viewer that anything out of the ordinary is going on. One has to scan the green water closely to find it. There, low in the composition and off center, is a tiny V shape painted in wispy white. The filmy V looks a little like the blade end of an open scissors or a pair of crossed feathers dropped into the waves. The little V is, of course, the legs of Icarus about to be swallowed up by the sea. One could look at the picture a long time, even move on, without noticing any sign of Icarus in the composition.

The Renaissance masters helped to record the emerging modern view of experience. By contrast in Ovid's account of Daedalus and Icarus being viewed by those on land, the flying pair *were* amazing, focal and wondrous. It is the modern commitment to civil order and purpose that turns away from the drama of the puer.

Contemporary attempts to paint out or marginalize the puer spirit beyond conscious acknowledgment involve, in one way or another, relegating it to pathology. Doing so requires establishing first a theory of normal personality development in which each child is seen to pass through a progression of known stages. These might be the psychosexual stages of Freud and Erikson, the cognitive stages of Piaget, or the moral stages of Kohlberg. As held by the educational establishment, these stage theories tend to meld into one, and once accepted, the validity of the underlying premises is no longer questioned. As one modern educational critic puts it, educators now think "with" the underlying assumptions of stage theory—not "about" those assumptions. The most critical of these is that children move unidirectionally from a primitive, concrete experience of the world to a discerning, socially adaptive one. Also fundamental to developmental theory is that each stage is adjacent to the next; a child must pass from the first to the second to the third, and so on, with no capricious leaps ahead. Preschools, educational institutions, and enlightened home environments are designed to facilitate developmental progress through what are believed to be age-appropriate stages. There are, of course, genetic deficiencies, trauma-induced arrests, breakdowns in nurturance or in the school program, and these account for the children—a great majority of them boys—who fail to make acceptable developmental progress. Such children are summarily considered developmentally impaired. Their difference from the norms of their age and stage are clinically named and described. There are learning disorders, and there are affective disorders. Therapies, remediation programs, and, most recently, psychoactive drugs are prescribed to restore the developmentally impaired child to the norms of his stage. Prosperous, enlightened families and communities expend enormous resources to achieve satisfactory child development. Impoverished, neglected families and communities cannot do this, and their children fail to thrive, even become feral, "street children."

The developmental system, however, is a closed system. Its end product is a socially and economically adaptable contributor to the established civil order. There is no place in it for the transcendent boy: the savant, seer, savior, hero, avatar of another world. In the developmental system, to attend to anything but what is prescribed and approved is to have an "attention deficit." To turn one's head, to reach out to, to run to what most intensely engages one's spirit is a sign of unacceptable "hyperactivity." A child who senses the deadening encroachment of too much restriction, too great a denial of what is life-giving and thrilling is likely to haul a protective blanket over the spark of vitality he knows and trusts. In this spirit-preserving cocoon he is very likely to be diagnosed as depressive, perhaps autistic to some degree, a sufferer of Asperger's syndrome. If sufficiently remediated or medicated, he may pass, or appear to pass, developmental tests. In this vision there are no truly divergent children. The ultimate allegiance of nurturers and educators is to the developmental system, not the child. In such a system, no one is likely to see, as Auden wrote, "something amazing," a boy falling out of the sky.

Apart from the rebellious and reckless young, the culturally disenfranchised, and the mad, it might be thought that, even within the civil order, certain kinds of truth seekers—philosophers, depth psychologists— would keep an eye out for the living puer. Jung may be said to have done so, as have some of his distinguished disciples in archetypal psychology, notably Marie-Louise von Franz and James Hillman. In fact, during the 1959–60 winter semester of the Jung Institute in Zurich, von Franz gave a series of twelve interactive lectures titled, tellingly, *The Problem of the Puer Aeternus*. Moreover, she establishes from the outset that the "problem" is not in understanding or appreciating the phenomenon of the puer figure; the problem lies, rather, in the waste and wreckage of lives lived in the puer mode. Very much in the spirit of her age, von Franz begins with an equation of puer qualities and pathological maladjustment: "In general, the man who is identified with the archetype of the *puer aeternus* remains too long in adolescent psychology; that is, all those characteristics that are normal in a youth of seventeen or eighteen are continued into later life, coupled in most cases with too great a dependence on the mother."[2]

Having established a diagnosis of pathology, von Franz goes on to reveal its manifestations. The mother-dependent puer is likely to grow into either an effeminate homosexual or a heterosexual Don Juan. The Don Juan response, she writes, is accompanied by an adolescent "romantic" attitude. In addition, the puer-spirited individual exhibits a "false individualism," which liberates him from ordinary social conformity. He is likely to feel himself a "hidden genius." Vacillating between deep feelings of inferiority and arrogance, he has an impossible time determining the right job or the right partner. His given reality is always critically lacking in some essential way. From his own interior perspective, the puer-dominated individual feels he has not yet arrived in his real, destined life. For this reason, he cannot fully enter any given moment. He may well feel that he is a savior, a prophet, a messiah. The puer figure's ultimate dread, von Franz maintains, is to be bound by any kind of commitment. Stable living and working conditions are experienced inwardly as a kind of hell. There is a powerful drive to slip out of them and to escape. The escape, von Franz continues, is often into what are now called extreme sports. Flying and mountaineering are favored—"so as to get as high as possible"[3]—and many puer figures die in crashes and falls.

Having laid out the seriousness of the puer pathology, von Franz then steps back to acknowledge some of the stimulating positivity that the puer spirit looses in the world.

> In general the positive quality of such youths is a certain kind of spirituality which comes from a relatively close contact with the unconscious. Many have the charm of youth and the stirring quality of a drink of champagne. [*Puer aeterni*] are generally very agreeable to talk to. They usually have interesting things to talk about and have an invigorating effect on one. They do not like conventional situations; they ask deep questions and go straight for the truth.[4]

These are surprisingly endearing and important qualities to be associated with such a dire pathology. Aware of this, von Franz remarks on her own negativity, qualifying it as a picture of the puer "if viewed superficially," by which she means from the standpoint of ordinary civic sensibility. What really intrigues her, she announces, is why the puer is becoming such a frequent and prominent figure at that historical moment: "It seems to me that the problem of the *puer aeternus* is becoming increasingly actual."[5] As the Western world hovered on the brink of what would be a spectacular eruption of youthful counterculture, von Franz speculated that the puer-spirited youth may be arising as the dominant "problem" of the age.

Because, to her mind, the puer presence was a syndrome and a "problem," she believed it required a cure. Though "curing" a puer-spirited person is an uncertain prospect at best, von Franz drew on Jung's thinking, in *Symbols of Transformation,* to prescribe conventional hard work. Positing puer flightiness and unworldliness as the symptoms, sustained work as the cure, von Franz saw no easy resolution. The puer, she acknowledges, will fly from any sustained tedium. He will quit, pack up, and look elsewhere. How can one argue the case for the tedious, the repetitive, the workaday—the "middle course"—to one who cannot bear it, whose spirit is alive with intimations of ecstatic, higher things? Appropriately enough, von Franz sought deeper understanding in an investigation of the life of Saint-Exupéry.

Von Franz notes at the outset of her analysis that Saint-Exupéry's life is "difficult to trace," and that this elusiveness is characteristic of puer types. This forgivably inaccurate assessment is due to the fact that substantial biographical studies and memoirs were not yet published at the time of her lectures. The sketchiness of the facts at her disposal did not deter her from speculating that there may have been something of the "Nazi psychology" at work in Saint-Exupéry, a tendency to alternate between sentimentality and brutality. No other writers, however, including intimate friends, lovers, his wife, or such fastidious biographers as Stacy Schiff, detected any "brutality" in the man. As suggested in the previous chapter, he did, without question, embrace a polyamorous approach to women, but he did not exhibit the characteristic Don Juanist qualities von Franz suggests. He was remarkably loyal both to lovers and to his wife, seemingly constitutionally unable to discard or to devalue them. Moreover, erratic and eccentric as he was on the job, he worked for sustained periods and very hard at both his flying and his writing. Discussing the proclivity of puer types for flying, von Franz advances the thesis that "most airmen do not want to fly after they have reached the age of thirty." This was clearly not the case with Saint-Exupéry, whose desire to fly did not flag even when beset by dangerous prospects and terrible physical discomfort.

Von Franz is on her most solid ground in her explication of *The Little Prince* and what it reveals about its author. She rightly recognizes that the downed flyer who narrates the tale is a Saint-Exupéry alter ego, and his whimsically remembered childhood as a failed artist represents the existential problem of how to "pull out of this fantasy life of youth and youthfulness without losing its value." In recognizing the difficulty of this dilemma, von Franz realizes that the "fantasy life of youth"—the puer spirit—is an intrinsic value, not a passing condition.

> The great problem is that you can drive people out of their childhood paradise and fantasy life, in which they are in close connection with their true inner self at an infantile level, but then they are completely disillusioned and cynical.
>
> . . . One can drive away both devils *and* angels by saying all is infantile.[6]

Von Franz is at once perplexed and challenged by Saint-Exupéry. Probably unwittingly she calls him, at one point in her lectures, an undeniable genius and a great writer, noting elsewhere that he was probably neither. Having begun by forcefully establishing him as a defective, incompletely realized being, held pathologically in the puer complex, she must contend in *The Little Prince* with an artist-persona vividly aware of his puer spirit. Indeed, the narrator is so consciously aware of his puer that he embodies it symbolically in the figure of the little prince so that the narrator can, literally and figuratively, embrace him and consign the adult-puer relationship to deep understanding. Even as she lectures, von Franz cannot help but shift her ground; her very analysis of *The Little Prince* seems to suggest that Saint-Exupéry may himself have artfully solved the problem she is addressing.

The child motif when it turns up represents a bit of spontaneity, and the great problem—in each case an ethical and individual one—is to decide whether it is now an infantile shadow which has to be cut off and repressed, or something creative moving toward a future possibility of life.[7]

To her credit, von Franz admits that it is sometimes impossible to determine the difference between an infantile regression and a spiritual tug in the direction of fuller personal realization. Finally, she wonders about, but does not claim to know, the truth of the situation with Saint-Exupéry.

For one cannot (or at least I cannot) make up one's mind whether to treat the figure of the little prince as a destructive infantile shadow whose apparition is fatal and announces Saint Exupéry's death, or to treat it as the divine spark of his creative genius.[8]

In subsequent lectures this ambivalence reverts to decided certainty of pathology rather than genius. In this frame of mind von Franz writes that Saint-Exupéry's "art is very neurotic," adding that "it is doubtful that he is a great artist." She is openly antagonistic to the celebrity he achieved after his death—"such a fuss is made about him"—and speculates that his adulation "might be looked upon as an expression of the neuroses of the present day."

Whatever von Franz believed to be the "neuroses" the troubled youth of the hour were expressing, she is not willing to see in it any truly revolutionary or redemptive spark. Although Saint-Exupéry's *The Little Prince* sets forth the puer's relationship to adult consciousness with great clarity—and with powerful emotional effect—she refuses finally to accept it. Puzzlingly, given the obvious artfulness of the tale, she speculates that the forty-three-year-old author was not really "conscious" of what he had written. To have concluded otherwise would have been to concede to Saint-Exupéry a penetration and vision perhaps exceeding that of analytical psychology. And it is finally to her theoretical science that von Franz gives her highest allegiance. Under the lens of archetypal psychology, Saint-Exupéry's life, work, and message must remain a "problem." The material, not the analytic system, is determined to be defective, and the principal defect is a lack of "psychology."

> I think that if he had got in touch—and this is awfully optimistic—but if he had come into touch with psychology, something might have been done with his problem, because he was very near to finding the solution himself, but somehow, tragically enough, he lived in this kind of light French milieu where there is absolutely no psychological understanding yet at work.[9]

Something at work in von Franz wants to find definitive fault with Saint-Exupéry. As both example and champion of the puer-spirited type, he is easily made to typify the entire puer "problem." Here, as von Franz notes with some candor, special difficulties arise, as Saint-Exupéry led a remarkably rich and realized life. He vividly imagined flight, and then—spectacularly, dangerously, thrillingly—he flew. In flight he felt that he had, like a dreaming boy, transcended earthbound banality and heaviness. Cloaked, literally, in stars, he was present in another world, a golden world. He was a great and appreciative friend. He took great pleasure in carefree, congenial company, and he enjoyed plenty of it. He ate heartily and drank deeply. Most of his books and journalism were warmly received and publicly honored. He was a devoted son and brother and, in an admittedly eccentric way, a devoted husband. He saw a great deal of the world—five continents—from the land and from the air. He lost things he treasured, suffered, rebounded. He died a hero's death, in service of his country. His impact and influence, especially that of *The Little Prince*, continues to be felt in the world. If Saint-Exupéry's life represents a "problem," it is a problem millions might yearn to experience.

Psychology can firmly consign Saint-Exupéry and the puer-type generally to the ranks of the pathological if it can locate in such figures a deep and unnecessary morbidity. While Saint-Exupéry risked his life many times before finally losing it, there is little in his written work or in his recorded conversation or behavior to suggest any such tendency. Von Franz looks for it in the little prince's fatal arrangement with the yellow snake. She sees in this a predisposition to depart early from the world, a refusal to partake of it fully and to commit to its requirements. Yet the little prince's passing is narrated briefly and with great delicacy. For him, the lethal bite will not be a termination of his being, but a passage back to his asteroid home and to his beloved rose. From the narrator's perspective, again, the departure of the little prince is a great sadness—but it is an endurable sadness because the little prince has taught him the mysterious truth that it is the invisible realities that make the visible ones beautiful. So, far from morbid, the loss of the little prince leaves both narrator and reader with a sense of enlightened serenity.

But even this serenity can be configured into the "problem" of the puer. Explicating the little prince's fatal encounter with the snake and its aftermath, von Franz writes:

It is really Saint Exupéry who should have been poisoned; that would have detached him from the little prince. . . .

The *puer aeternis* very often has this natural, detached attitude towards life, which is normal for old people but which he acquires prematurely—the idea of that life is not everything, that the other side is valid too, that life is only part of the whole of existence.[10]

From this perspective, a life imaginatively and sometimes ecstatically lived is problematic. It is a "problem" even when it reveals intimations of such transporting beauty and meaning that the dread of death loses its power to dispirit or terrify. This, at any rate, is the considered view of Marie-Louise von Franz and perhaps of psychological science generally. It fittingly encompasses the view of the ascending Icarus, observed from the ground.

# 7

## ICARUS AND THE GOLDEN WORLD

TRANSPORTED IN FLIGHT, Icarus ascended up toward the radiant sun, leaving everything—his father and the glittering earth—below. Sensing heaven, what could bind him to Crete or Athens or to a "middle course?" The puer spirit always senses heaven, and the call is always irresistible. Sometimes, too, the puer-spirited leave stirring and unforgettable accounts of what they find.

The Jungian analyst and writer Robert Johnson experienced heaven—what he would call the Golden World—at several formative moments in his remarkable life, and as he approached his eightieth year, he made an account of those experiences in his memoir, *Balancing Heaven and Earth*.

Like Icarus, Johnson had his initial intimation of heaven's call when he himself had arisen out of his own health and safety and hovered between life and death. He was eleven years old and living in Portland, Oregon. His mother and father had divorced, and in the aftermath he lived in a rooming house kept by his mother across town from his father, who lived alone. On Saturdays his routine was to bicycle to his father's rooms, visit for an hour or so, and bicycle back home. Returning from one such visit on an especially hot Saturday, he decided to stop halfway at a shop and buy a soda. Just as he was entering the shop there was a terrible collision on the street, and one of the vehicles crashed into the doorway he was entering. The errant car caught one of his legs and mangled it so badly he was rushed to the hospital, where the ruined lower leg was amputated. Late that night, as he lay bandaged and alone in his hospital bed, he was aware of a strange sensation. Beneath the dressings, something had gone wrong with the sealing of the wound, and he was hemorrhaging badly. He remembers feeling, with serene lucidity, his vital essence escaping his body. This realization was accompanied by a profound and welcome feeling that he was being assumed into a great, tranquil, higher order of being.

I was slowly bleeding to death, and I began drifting away to another world. I knew precisely what was happening, at least in its psychic dimensions. I set my feet against the downward spiral and determined not to die, resisting it with all my willpower. But at a specific moment I crossed a divide—it felt like that bump against the doorjamb—and suddenly I was in a glorious world.

It was pure light, gold, radiant, luminous, ecstatically happy, perfectly beautiful, purely tranquil, joy beyond bound. I wasn't the least bit interested in anything on the earthly side of the divide; I could only revel at what was before me . . .

But I was not to leave this earthly world on that August day in 1932; instead I was only to be teased with a brief preview of the Golden World that would figure so profoundly throughout the rest of my life. An alert night nurse came by and noticed blood leaking through the underside of my cast. She set off an alarm and had me whisked off to surgery, where they quickly tried to transfuse blood. My veins were so badly collapsed that I still have ribbons of white scars down my arms where they made incisions, searching desperately to find a vein.

Inwardly, I was harshly interrupted in my timeless ecstasy of paradise by a summons to go back to the earthly realm. I resisted this as strenuously as I had fought the crossing from earth to heaven, but to no avail. I awoke on the surgery table convulsed with pain, hearing the busy sounds of an emergency room, and looking up into a nightmare of tubes and a circle of masked faces peering down at me. One of these, the surgeon, said, "So, you are alive!"

Yes, I was alive but reluctantly so. No one can look upon even the antechamber of heaven without a lifetime of regret at what has been lost.[1]

Five years later when he was sixteen, he had another life-altering encounter with the Golden World. Because of his artificial leg and perhaps because he had been an introverted and cerebral boy, he had not yet held a real job, a "man's" job. Therefore in the summer of his sixteenth year, in the heart of the Depression, he signed on to work the night shift at a nearby tomato-canning factory. His first night on the job may have been the darkest, most hellish night of his life.

I was just getting the hang of my new job when the night foreman decided to pirate labor to help with a bottleneck farther down the production line. My job of inspecting cans was expendable. I knew nothing of fending for myself in the work world, and I soon found myself on one of the most grueling jobs in the factory, hand-trucking four-hundred-pound loads of hot cans from cooker to warehouse. I had never been near a two-wheeled hand truck before, let alone one with cans stacked high above my head that had to be carefully balanced. With my first venture I spilled the entire stack of cans across the floor and was roundly chewed out by the foreman. I wasn't very strong, and the job was far beyond my ability, but I was too determined to admit defeat. I clung to the task at hand and decided that this was a true test of my manhood: either I was going to prove myself or die in the attempt. As the night wore on it was nearly the latter.

I spent the next six hours pushing that hand truck from one end of the building to the other. Sometime after midnight I was given a short break, and I was relieved when the foreman assigned the job to someone else. But after my break he sent me back to the same exhausting task, and again I went to it without saying a word. By this time the junction of my leg and the artificial leg was soaked with blood. The blood had run down into my shoe, and my wool sock was so wet that you could have wrung it out, but I prided myself on not complaining to anyone. This was my test, and I was going to do it or die. I don't know what was worse—the pain from my leg or my first untempered look at the harshness and ugliness of the world. They merged together in my mind into pure misery.[2]

Spiritually spent and physically bloodied, he knew he could not return directly home. He felt he needed to meditate on something green, something natural, if only to efface the sickening impression of the brutal night in the airless confines of the canning factory.

At 4:30 A.M. I punched my time card and walked out into the damp night air. As I started my borrowed car I suddenly realized that if I didn't see something beautiful I would not survive. I needed to get home, soak in a bathtub, and collapse into bed, but another need was even more powerful. I had to have the beauty of life confirmed again, or I felt that I could not continue to live. I drove up into the hills west of Portland, where I knew I would find a view overlooking the valley, reaching to the four snowcapped mountains that surround the city. This was my answer to the compelling need for something to counterbalance the horror of the preceding hours.

I parked the car and hobbled out onto a promontory just in time for the sunrise. The sun began to inch its way over the horizon, and—unbelievably—the Golden World shone forth again with all its glory. The same world I had known at age eleven, the same golden light, the same condensation of pure beauty—it was all there. It was the same world that I had lost and mourned several years before, and I knew it with an intimacy and delight past any other value in human life.[3]

So there it was again, confirmed. Johnson knew he could not hold the Golden World fast and summon it back at will, but periodically thereafter it would summon him. He had experienced the Golden World, he felt, for a reason, and the experiences were so insistent that he felt his life would be pointless and empty if he dedicated himself to any other pursuit than to integrate these visions into his understanding and into his waking life. The Golden World was thereafter the fixed spiritual point in relation to which all his crucial life decisions were referenced. To the degree to which his subsequent experience resonated with intimations of the Golden World, he pursued that course; when he could feel no such resonance, he ceased the deadening activity at hand and waited. The story of his life carried out in this highly intuitive, interior manner is, to my reading, more fantastic and surprising than the course of any novel by Dickens or Robertson Davies. Periodically intimating what he calls "slender threads" descending from the Golden World, Johnson made his gnomic and improbable way from university to the spiritual community of Krishnamurti, to Zurich and the Jung Institute, to Southern California and India, between which he has divided his adult life. Reading the unaffected account of his attempts to reconcile, literally, heavenly and earthly experience is to encounter a life lived truly out of the historical moment in which he was placed.

There is actually ample witness to the call of the Golden World in the literary record. In his stirringly anthropopathic stories of dogs, Jack London identified it as the call of the wild: an urgent sense of vitality and connectedness to a pre-civilized, prehuman condition before consciousness was imposed on sheer animal being. In his spiritual memoir, *Surprised by Joy*, C. S. Lewis recounts being overcome with an all-being rapture when, as a boy, he read Norse mythology and the metaphysical adventure stories of George MacDonald. He called the beckoning otherness his "northernness" and, like Robert Johnson, dedicated his inner life thereafter to understanding its relationship to its outer circumstances.

As suggested at the outset of the previous chapter, the revelation of a Golden World just behind the scrim of practical life is the message of all the "secret garden" literature discussed in Humphrey Carpenter's study by that name. In those stories there is always a puer at play, or longing to be. Children do not need a panoramic backdrop of vastness or wilderness to be drawn into the Arcadian Golden World—although vastness and wilderness are most welcome. It takes no more physical space or verdure or light than can be found in an actual garden or a quiet spot by a streambed. A. A. Milne's "three-acre wood" was world enough for Christopher Robin and Pooh. Frank L. Baum's Oz and J. M. Barrie's Neverland are treasured evocations of the Golden World, but they are, like accounts of the biblical heaven told to children, a permanently separate realm from "real life." Only a fortuitous cyclone or a magical sprinkling of fairy dust can grant passage. Stories of that magical passage are charming to children, but the very fancifulness of the accounts helps the child to relegate the stories and the feelings they evoke to make believe and just pretend.

For this very reason, stories that show nonmagical continuity between waking world and Golden World leave an even deeper and more hopeful imprint on the heart of a child. In Kenneth Grahame's *The Wind in the Willows,* for example, the Golden World is more than a benign and sunny stretch of riverbank, meadow, and copse in the English countryside. Those lovingly rendered features are in fact irradiated by the golden, transformative Presence that Robert Johnson beheld at twenty as dawn broke over the ridge before him. Most of *Wind in the Willows* is an account of mildly humorous adventures of the principal characters, Ratty, Mole, Badger, Toad. But the strongest and most arresting tale is recounted in the chapter, "The Piper at the Gates of Dawn," in which the rodent friends go off in pursuit of Otter's lost son, who has disappeared somewhere along the riverbank. As the animals navigate Ratty's boat through the reeds of the river, the urgency of finding the lost and vulnerable child recedes as the passengers are overcome by the transporting presence of divinity-in-nature.

Slowly, but with no doubt or hesitation whatever, and in something of a solemn expectancy, the two animals passed through the broken, tumultuous water and moored their boat at the flowery margin of the island. In silence they landed, and pushed through the blossom and scented herbage and undergrowth that led up to the level ground, till they stood on a little lawn of a marvelous green, set round with Nature's own orchard-trees—crabapple, wild cherry, and sloe.

"This is the place of my song-dream, the place the music played to me," whispered the Rat as if in a trance. "Here, in this holy place, here if anywhere, surely we shall find Him!"

Then suddenly the Mole felt a great Awe fall upon him, an awe that turned his muscles to water, bowed his head, and rooted his feet to the ground. It was no panic terror—indeed he felt wonderfully at peace and happy—but it was an awe that smote and held him and, without seeing, he knew it could only mean that some august Presence was very, very near . . . and then, in that utter clearness of the imminent dawn, while Nature, flushed with fullness of incredible colour, seemed to hold her breath for the event, he looked in the very eyes of the Friend and Helper; saw the backward sweep of the curved horns, gleaming in the growing daylight; saw the stern, hooked nose between the kindly eyes that were looking down on them humorously, while the bearded mouth broke into a half-smile at the corners; saw the rippling muscles on the arm that lay across the broad chest, the long supple hand still holding the pan-pipes only just fallen away from the parted lips; saw the splendid curves of the shaggy limbs disposed in majestic ease on the sward; saw, last of all, nestling between his very hooves, sleeping soundly in entire peace and contentment, the little, round, podgy, childish form of the baby otter. All this he saw, for one moment breathless and intense, vivid on the morning sky; and still, as he looked, he lived; and still, as he lived, he wondered.[4]

For Grahame, the Golden World was not held in a forever inaccessible Arcadian past, nor was it consigned to a metaphysical above-and-beyond: Oz, Neverland, Heaven. The Golden World was there, even Pan the eternal puer was there, just along the river, right where they lived. Not insignificantly, the rescuers are granted this experience of the Presence while in pursuit of a child lost and in peril.

There seem to be no geographical requirements for a glimpse into the Golden World. Saint-Exupéry, the first time he was downed in the Sahara and waiting alone in the dunes for his flying mates to return for him, recalled a wonderful aura of light at day's end. As a gazelle entered the golden light, Saint-Exupéry was overcome with a surpassing sense of peacefulness and self-sufficiency: the first time, he reported, that he realized "his life was his own" and that he was responsible for it.

About twenty years ago, when I was in my thirties, I wrote and published a novel, *The Headmaster's Papers,* and almost immediately afterward felt an insistent urge to start another kind of book. Neither my age nor my life achievements seemed to call for a "memoir," but I was agitated to write something that was "true." More specifically, I felt the need to report a certain quality of experience that, in my limited investigation, was undocumented or chronicled elsewhere. The truth is, I did not really have a clear idea of what I wanted to achieve in this book, but I set out to do it anyway. A vivid flood of early childhood and boyhood memories returned to me, as if they had somehow been dammed up and waiting. I duly wrote them down in a series of very long, intense sittings. The writing came easily, and I was gratified that, without seeming to labor the process, the events assumed the shape of stories, stories which, though highly personal and a little strange, I hoped might be interesting to others. The manuscript bewildered its eventual publisher and some of its editors, but with a few misgivings on their part, it appeared as a book, *Seeing Things: A Chronicle of Surprises.*

The publisher's uneasiness about the project proved to be justified, as the book received only a few reviews, and not many copies were sold. Only recently has it occurred to me what I had been attempting to express in that book and what had caused it to take shape in the unorthodox way that it did. I see now that I was trying to recount, serially, my own intimations of the Golden World. Some were encounters with other children and people who seemed to radiate such vivid importance—unrelated to their social importance—that they were to me more like angels from another order than they were mere schoolmates or neighbors. I tried very hard, for example, to convey the astonishing, charged quality of certain girls that made me love them with an intensity for which I had—then— no words or gestures to express. I tried also, in *Seeing Things*, to express the obsessive allure of seemingly all animals, even animals I wanted to hunt and kill.

*The prairie—we called it The Fields—was an early confirmation of divinity-on-earth.*

*Hiking, crawling, bellying under and over the fields of high grass, the creek banks, the marshy thickets of sumac and scrub, I understood the primitive impulse to* map out *turf. The retreading of familiar steps, especially in a wilderness, serves to imprint that turf in the brain. External geography is not real until it becomes internal geography. I charted an intricate expanse that covered miles of fields beyond the town's edge, knew every thicket, every tractor path, the depth and feel of each bend in the creek, knew which of the slender scrub trees would support a climber's weight and which tangle of bush and branch was waste and which was likely to give up a crazed rabbit.*

*And there were those breathtaking stands of poplars (planted in such straight lines to demarcate property?) against deep blue late afternoon skies— or—sometimes, against orange-pink sunset, which, when it happens, is pure holiness. What are those poplars about? They seem to me now to be about France, about forgotten, quiet times when rural people went about their business, worlds away from Caesar or Charlemagne or Napoleon. A chapter in the Ancient Rome book my students read is called "The Long Twilight." It is a rich and full account of how in the provincial parts of the politically hopeless*

*Empire—Britain south of the Wall, Gaul west of the Rhine, and in all the rolling, habitable places south of the Danube—life went on, even prosperously, even sweetly. Along the East Anglian fens, across the dusk-lit fields of Brittany, provincial souls surely ached with the fullness of the long twilight: gazing at and beyond stands of poplars on the horizon.*

*The fields beyond the edge of town were glutted with animals—not deer, which the farmers had cajoled and herded into forest preserves regulated by the state of Illinois. But the animals that are part of the texture of the prairie itself are indomitable: buckwheat-colored rabbits, squirrels, chucks, muskrats, possum, skunk, shaggy rats, river rats, chipmunks, field mice, black snakes, garter snakes, and corn snakes. Because our fields were not farmed or cut, they would, on hot, dry, July mornings, shiver and hiss with snakes starting and twisting away from our footsteps: a glimpse only of their khaki and stripes through the bleached swirls of grass. Khaki and stripes—they all wore the same clothes: chipmunk, garter, toad, grasshopper, badger, beaver, even the forgotten fawn.*

*At his—at my—core the boy is, like Narcissus at his pool, trying to get back to something, trying to join it, merge with it. Spring thaws the impulse; July excites it to boiling. Boy's eye meets bird's eye with an inarticulate thrill, moves to it, would hold it in his hands if he could. He would—and this is true—kill it.*

*Killing is a little-investigated expression of the impulse to have. Thoreau knew about it. He said he would never trust a pacifist who had not evolved through his urge to hunt. Every boy at his core knows the urge. I am not sure that girls know it.*

*Killing is an extension of sweet desire, or a primal love—which sounds wretched, perverse. Moreover, it is wretched and perverse, the impulse spoiled the instant it becomes understood: when it becomes a conscious intention. Only in deep alienation, in the most depressed illnesses and in the cheapest "art" is the self-conscious killing of the beloved celebrated as profound. But for boys, for a spell in their time, the desire for animals and the desire to kill them are fused. So sweet and so deeply pulsing is the fusion that civilized restraints on its expression (although very important for civilization) do not diminish it in the least. The drive overpowers restraint, overpowers gentler affections. It spills over its bearer, and it spills over the living objects of desire. It can so overcome the killer that even the means of killing—the dagger, the bow, the arrow, the rifle—become charged with it.* Men even now, arrested here, make idols of their weapons. They oil stocks. They sift bullets through their fingers like coins. They feel, and even dully express, that the sweetness, the power is somehow in the gun. *Potential slaughter lies this way, and it has always lain that way.*

*The boy's eye instantly closes the distance between self and the bird on the wire. The rabbit hounded out of bramble and zigzagging wildly out of reach is frozen in the boy's mind's eye. There is furry fold between the shoulder and the neck, a soft vulnerability, a target.*

*Imaginary hunts preoccupy the boy at rest. Simulated hunts fill his play. Halting, hopeless, half-understood hunts direct his wandering through prairie and thicket. There may be a gun, toy or not. There may be a longing for a gun.*

*Before the rifle (smuggled against permission into the garage) there was a year of the bow and arrow.* Father—what a lapse! *The bow was as tall as I was, and I could string it only with arm-trembling exertions. The four blue-feathered, silver-tipped arrows I quickly lost, shot past all finding in the fields, and replacements were purchased at the hardware store in town.* Merchants—where did you imagine those arrows would fly? *Into straw-backed targets? Into cardboard boxes? No, they were fired dreamily up into the undersides of eagles, dead into the swollen guts of bears. Rabbits, foxes, and weasels were stuck clear through, dead instantly, as if frozen by the arrow shafts.*

*There were never enough arrows. Two or three were bounty. A shot into the fields, if it was a shot of any distance, was almost certainly a lost arrow. Yet every afternoon of a late, cold, darkening autumn friend and I, equally entranced by the lure of the kill, padded over the frosty tufts of prairie grass, our toes, fingertips, noses raw with the cold. The lower the sun behind the poplars and behind the ravaged stalks of corn, the creamier the grassy way before us. In that light the swirls of spent grasses were transformed from tans to peach to rose. Only a few times did I see the full cycle into soft grays and blues as night fell. (These outings entailed, besides the loss of supper, angry reprisals and promised confinements.)*

*What were we expecting with our numbing fingers wrapped around the* varnished curve of our bows, our two or three mangy arrows rattling over our backs in their makeshift quivers? We expected deer. We expected a majestic buck. He would step unexcitedly out of a thicket and pause before us, the hoof of one foreleg raised slightly above the turf. He would see us but look beyond us. Then our arrows would pierce him, would make him ours. We could know this passionately, relegating the knowledge of forest preserves to the insubstantial realm of common sense and recent history.

There is a margin of time at dusk on a prairie—the hour when tans blur into rose—when a deer, when even a lion, could emerge before a boy. But in spite of this knowledge we were frightened almost senseless when, in the course of stalking noisily over some spent corn rows, not one, not two, but three pheasants, pheasants rampant, roared up out of the stubble right in front of us. I knew as I drew back my arrow (far too late) that I was no match for the pheasants' magnificence. I might just as well have thrown my arrows at them or made a face. Once projected up into the darkening blue, the pheasants became pure silhouette and glided off in a great arc. Far behind them, far too low, our arrows rose, wobbled, and fell back to earth, lost in a thick stand of scrub. Waves of feeling-reverence and loss—silenced us. We made a show of looking for our lost arrows, but it was rapidly darkening, and it was very cold. My friend said he had to go home; we were both inexcusably late.

I would not go. I was near tears, and I could not explain it. I was there, I had arrived, I was standing plumb in the middle of rosy, mythic light I had longed for. Three magnificent fowl, shimmering like honey in green, in deep red, had risen like flags to confirm it, and I had failed even to touch it. Another great bird arose. Before I reached for my last arrow, I knew how futile my "shot" would be; the very realization weakened my arms and my trembling fingers. Once again my arrow arched feebly below the trajectory of the pheasant. If I could not touch these things, I cried out loud, why was I there?

That night I could not sleep for the obsessive reconstruction of the first pheasants' rising. Even in imagination, I could not hold the bow still, could not hold the birds still against the stained glass sky and propel my loving shot through the bones of their breasts. I had been there, but I was just a boy with a boy's bow and two cheap arrows.[5]

Like Robert Johnson, I sometimes experienced the Presence, or
Golden World, in actual, assignable places. One such experience continues to revisit me. It occurred in the course of two hikes while on a
family vacation in the north woods of Michigan:

*One midsummer in the north of Michigan it all came back to me. My family
had taken a vacation cottage on a clear, cold lake. I had reached an age, twelve,
where Michigan no longer meant the tug of pike far beneath the glassy surface
of gold-brown water. The sharp-sweet pine, the tang of which, mixed with earth,
damp and cooking, rose up and tantalized me even inside the cabin. It was in
the sheets, in the sofa cushions, in the sink drains. It would emanate from the
walls and from the wide planks of the floor.*

*Other things had come up, unsettlingly, to command my attention: less sub-
stantial but more insistent. There were, foremost, the inexhaustible rituals of
sport. Each sport—baseball, golf, tennis—held out its own elaborate conventions, its attractive (but always subtly changing) nuances, and its gallery of local,
national, and mythic heroes. Not to mention the equipment. Sculptures in oiled
leather, miraculously polished wooden shafts and frames, gleaming club-heads,
somehow both bulbously heavy and sharp-edged, bottle-handled bats, creamy
new baseballs, the cul-de-sac of the cowhide's red stitches blurring into my concentration just before my air-creasing swing. Every summer morning opened into
the swirl and drill and news of sports, but the North Woods was not the place
for it; the North Woods suspended the noise.*

*One still and steamy afternoon there, left alone while the rest of the fam-
ily fished, I struck out aimlessly on a footpath into the woods. Without looking, eyes on the path, I passed beyond the ring of cottages, through the thick,
low pines, through gradations of terrain hardly noticed until I reached more
open, airier ground. The trees were silver birches, and they flickered their higher
leaves like bright coins in the breezes. There was movement now. The ground
fell away on one side of the path, dropping into the bed of a fast and forceful stream. The stream pushed itself noisily over and around rocks and fallen
timber. In the shallows, dappled tan and white, the stream glossed over smooth
stones, then darkened into deeper pools of root-beer brown.*

*Mindlessly hurried along by the stream, I happened onto a wide, sandy flat, where the current splayed out to the width of a little river. Ahead of me the birches and scrub circled around and closed the path, but by fording the sandy shallows I could cross the stream and proceed into range after range of pale sand dunes, creamy-looking in the late afternoon night.*

*There, midstream, the clear water rippling over the soles of my shoes, something underneath the surface caught my eye. The floor of the streambed, seemingly composed of sand and stones, began to move beneath the water like a slow kaleidoscope of earth tones. There was a quick intimation of "other laws" taking hold. I did not resist. I watched with a thrill as a cluster of mottled rocks before me became sizable crayfish, which, perhaps disturbed by my step, scuttled over the sand away from me. Then, as if sent to verify my trespass and to file a report, the lacquered snouts of four or five brown trout appeared about an invisible circumference perhaps a yard from where I stood. They hovered there, in tense precision like a line of bombers. Their iridescent browns, honey, and spangles picked up perfectly the camouflage of the crayfish, of the afternoon light over the rippled surface, and the dappled bottom cover. Next, as if to reveal to the adjusted eye even more elemental components of stream, dark minnows began shooting like needles through the composition, drawn forward in delicate parallels, then veering sharply away, as if filings before an unseen magnet.*

*Anything seemed possible in that enchanted light, provided I did not take a step. How long did I stay? A few seconds? An hour and a half? However long, it was rosy twilight, the water gone to dark glass, by the time I sloshed onto the dune side of the stream. I was half-willing to proceed over the dunes to an unseen Lake Superior, even, if I could have expressed it, to the Nile or to Arcady. But I took only a step or two, for out of the scrub along the stream's edge appeared a lovely doe and her fawn, mute and regal. Again the intimation:* other laws.

*What happened next would surely have been surprising at another time. But in this particular procession of events in which stones had become crustaceans, leaves mantises, the blacker scars on the birches wizened bats, it seemed inevitable that other deer, what must have been a herd of deer, would materialize out of the scrub and take their stately places at the stream's edge. Even in zoos or when otherwise domesticated, deer call one fleetingly back to an earlier time. Each wants to say something, some gentle warning. As with cats, both genders are profoundly feminine. Deer have been hurt so much and for so long that they can only take flight or implore. There were about forty of them that evening. They were spaced along the curve of the stream. Each would drink silently, then draw back upright and still, alert to twilight signals available only to a deer.*

*There I stood in the middle of it: a secret open to me—and perhaps opening still. Would wolves come down to drink? Panthers? I could spoil it with a shout, with a stomp of my foot, with a splash. Who would believe it? Who would even share it with me? I walked home.*

*I wanted to explain it to my family later but got no further than describing the path. I did not know how to begin to tell the truth about it. The facts, the words I knew did not say enough: I saw a lot of crayfish and fish and deer. Not even a photograph would contain what I saw. I said I took a hike and that it was really great.*

*I deliberated hard about asking my family to return with me to the enchanted spot. Even now I am not sure whether the thing I dreaded most was that when we reached the ford, there would be nothing to see—or that they would see what I had seen, and the very fact of so much publicity would disenchant the experience forever. As it happened I did not take anybody to the spot, but I returned a few days later, alone.*

*I took off on this second solitary hike just after bright noon and wondered whether this would alter everything. The walk seemed longer. The path was muggy and buggy, but the gusts that brushed through the birches and the pines stirred up enough sense of deep solitude that another powerful transformation seemed at least possible. Would it be the same? Did I really want it to be the same?*

*Just at the point where the path terminated and, around a bend of scrub, the stream splayed out into the sandy flat, I stopped. Had it ever really happened? Had I dreamed all that life? The answer came crackling noisily from my left. A large doe shouldered her way out of the thick scrub and stopped still about ten yards ahead of me on the path. With the calm of a cow, she swung her head in my direction and appeared to consider me thoughtfully. Satisfied of something, she turned away and stepped unhurried around the bend to the rushing water. Satisfied myself, I ran home.*[6]

Once again, the book in which I recounted these and other Golden World sightings was far from a literary or commercial success, but it gratified me very much that some readers let me know in unmistakable ways that they understood and appreciated what I had reported—almost in the manner members of a secret, outlaw society might acknowledge a comrade: *Yes, I know, I'm one, too.*

It is difficult to imagine a setting less likely to dissolve into radiance of the Golden World than that of my school. My school at its best—and I believe it is often at its best—is, as described at the beginning of this book, a phenomenally busy, purposeful, and tightly scheduled place. In the climate of school, it is easy to feel certain about one's obligations, what constitutes success and failure, what is right and wrong. The longer one is immersed in it, the harder it is to imagine that there could be another realm of experience beyond and greater than its rigors, classes, and activities. School's calendar and bells come to mark the cadence of life more surely than the seasons. Because it is a bright and handsomely appointed place, situated in a forest and overlooking a placid pond, and because so many of the teachers and staff are accomplished, caring men and women who teach surely and well and who take a generous personal interest in their charges, it is only a rare and otherwise troubled boy who will experience the school as Robert Johnson experienced the tomato canning factory. But the very rightness of the place tends to close off the possibility of any other possible reality.

The boys in the school, especially those in the high school grades, seem to be well on their way to becoming men. Sometimes they reveal with unmistakable clarity that, along with their progress and accomplishments, they bear a great, confusing loss; there is a chronically sleepy, or sleepwalking, quality in such boys. Every now and again, in a poem or a picture or in a speech, a boy will give expression to a prior longing.

I will never forget one such occasion. It was a talk to the school given by one of the seniors as part of the required senior speaking program.

This particular boy was, from the faculty's standpoint, something of a cipher. A passable but undistinguished scholar, he held a needed job outside of school and was only lightly involved in sports and other school activities. He had the characteristically shaggy, slightly disheveled look of boys who are willing to meet only the technical requirements of the dress code. Reticent, but by no means difficult in class, he nonetheless enjoyed a kind of celebrity among his classmates. I remember feeling a kind of charged vibration among them as he rose to the podium to deliver his speech. As he did so, the hall was darkened for a videotaped movie he had made to illustrate his talk.

His subject was skateboarding, at which, the audience soon observed, he was phenomenally adept. I have no memory of what he said in the talk, as I, like everyone else in the audience, was transfixed by the video images. Quite a few of his classmates were aware of his skateboarding prowess, and the talk was broken by roars of appreciation. Because athletics are such a central and focal activity in the school, it has been easy for me to assess a boy's athleticism—even his vitality—on the basis of his performance on school teams. The world pictured in the skateboarding video bore no relationship to the world of uniformed athletes moving in elaborately structured concert to advance a ball, or to score goals.

I had never seen anything like this video. I had seen plenty of boys skittering about on their skateboards in parks and parking lots of the town where I lived, but this was nothing like that. This boy had mastered the art of riding his skateboard over the most improbable surfaces and inclines. I watched him poised and tilted on his board as he rode down steep stairways. His specialty seemed to be to ride the metal handrails of outdoor staircases. Surely, I assumed, he must have fallen many times in learning to pilot his board over rails scarcely wider than its wheels. One such fall, it appeared obvious, could have killed him, broken his neck. But no falls were recorded in the video, just one electrically tense descent after another. To me, now, the whole experience of the boy's presentation resolves into a single, indelible image. The video camera must have been held very close to the ground at the base of a long set of concrete steps. Boy and board had alighted on the tubular steel handrail at the top of the staircase, and halfway down the steep incline, the boy, his knees bowed and arms extended on each side, delicate as wings, flashed a bright, ecstatic smile. At just that instant, sunlight glinting off the rail created a flash that blanched the image white. There was an involuntary roar of—what?—approval, of affirmation from the boys in the audience. *There,* the image seemed to say, *there it is:* a boy in flight, in impossible flight, ecstatic, utterly sure of himself, in a world blanched white. To have seen it anywhere would have been stunning; to have seen it in school was a rare glimpse into the Golden World.

In the course of a young man's undergraduate years, he is likely to distance himself even further from the Golden World. From my recollection of my own college years in New England and from what I have observed of the college boys who graduate from my school, the *puer* spirit is likely to erupt in some form of dramatic regression before it is put behind them, perhaps forever.

For the great majority of boys, going away to college is the first sustained experience of living on their own. For more than a half century there has not really been a structure of adult supervision in place (*in loco parentis*) at most colleges and universities, and no matter what the rigors of the scholastic program, college boys find themselves radically free of prior restrictions. More than a few regress, break out wildly, test the new limits—and, without much reflection on how or why it happened, flunk out or burn out. Others are suspended for a time in what must objectively be considered a pre-civilized condition. They try drugs, eat and drink in binges, with no regard for their health. They let their clothes and bedding go without laundering. Out of the range of adult observation, they abandon all civility and decorum. Speech is reduced to coarse, repetitive vulgarities. As a previously unimaginable decadence becomes normative, they may take a manic delight in the condition, the kind of primitive shared hilarity celebrated, it seems to me with perfect pitch, in the now cult film, *Animal House*. In fact, when *Animal House* was first released in theaters, I went to see it because my students and still-in-touch former students told me it was "the funniest movie ever made," that it was "outrageous," that it was "perfect." The college setting of the film was eerily like the college I attended; moreover, it was set in the precise era of my undergraduate years. I can say without exaggeration that the feral, infantile, libidinous, and amoral antics of the film's principals were not "outrageous" in the sense of exaggerating reality. The Animal House of the film's title could have been any one of a number of similarly constituted fraternities at my college, including my own. The civic figures in the film—college dean, mayor, commandant of ROTC—were inflated and made cartoonish for comic effect, but the behavior, manner, and collective portrayal of the fraternity members was a faithful reconstruction of what I had seen and known. That my students found it "over the top," an outrageous spoof, gave me pause.

The enduring appeal of *Animal House* to boys in school is now clear to me. It is probably the very same, healing appeal provided by the medieval Feast of Fools, during which for a short, privileged, anarchic spell, the civic order could be turned festively upside down: the noble, the sacred, the pious, and the chaste could be mocked in a spirit of intoxicated hilarity; the mighty were cast down, and the fool was crowned king. In *Animal House,* young men on the brink of civic assimilation collectively refuse. The irrepressible impulsivity of boyhood shatters every pretension, butts its goatish head inside the bathroom door without knocking. It won't do any work or leave others alone to do theirs; it wants only to play, but not to play nicely. It wants to stick out its tongue, drop its pants, spit out its food. It wants to drop everything, pile into a car, speed off to a noisy dive where the drinking and dancing feel as if they might shake the place loose. And this is finally what all the rudeness and impulsiveness and convention-smashing and nose-thumbing are all about; they are an attempt to clear out every conventional and deadening obstacle to a self-obliterating, ecstatic party, a party that will not end. Nothing less—for a young man about to forsake his puer spirit for what can only appear to be the rest of his life—is required to reconnect him to the Golden World.

As much as the puer rises to the contours of ceremony and story, he is even quicker to sense a party. He is always at home at a real festival or celebration. Moreover—and this can be a problem—he knows no moderation. One's practical persona may claim to be content with a drink or two, a little novelty, and a modicum of agreeable company before departing the scene, but the puer wants more. He seeks, truth be told, the thrall of ecstasy, to thrum with the kind of transpersonal rapture kept firmly under wraps in the waking, working world. Under his influence, we seem dimly to recall primordial revels, a time and a feeling when all restraint has fallen away, when delight, surprise, unutterable beauty, orgasmic release, and delirium lay ahead. The puer's party knows no end except the end of one's life. The rapturous, all-out revel is very rarely realized, but its charged possibility skitters below, often just below, the chat and dance of ordinary convivial gatherings. There is a moment sometimes, when a party giddily lifts off. It could happen some Saturday night in someone's crowded living room, toward closing time at a neighborhood bar, in a rackety dance club, or on a tropical beach under the stars. The pitch and pace of the company's talk and movement rises and accelerates. Music, which may have been no more than periodically distracting, becomes elemental, hypnotic, a collective pulse. Mild disinhibition passes imperceptibly into intoxication. Then, all at once, the moment arrives. Someone has done something hilarious, outrageous. There are new, alluring arrivals. The gathering has become organic, the hive vibrating at a new, higher frequency. The atmosphere is shot through with sex, possibility, hilarity. However aroused, high, giddy, or glad the revelers feel, they are eager for more. They have surrendered, consecrated themselves to the party. This night there will be ritual communion, indulgence, trespass, danger. This night one is apt to do *anything*. And the puer seems to be saying, if it had words: yes, *at last!*

Many—who knows, perhaps even most—people live out the span of their lives without a single such party. Others experience one, two, or perhaps a few, awakening from them chastened and embarrassed. If the rapturous revel is treasured in memory at all, it tends to be relegated to the distant country of our youth or spirited young adulthood. Only the decadent and damned dwell continuously in the pulse of the party. The settled and stable, the civic minded, the modest and sensible, temperamental overforties, realists, the Moral Majority only rarely and inadvertently make a real party. They are never asked or welcome.

Men and women grow physically older and in time their energy declines. But the puer spirit neither ages nor tires. Vexing and unhelpful as it may be to one's practical well-being and to community, the puer knows and wants the transformation of a party.

Puer-spirited beings serve as messenger angels from the Golden World. Such beings are, in Robert Johnson's terms, "slender threads" connecting us to that higher, ecstatic condition. The problem perpetually facing the civic order is that both the puer and Golden World command, and command effortlessly, a higher allegiance. As such, the presence of the puer and glimpses and reports of a Golden World pose a serious threat to civil society. The civil order, it has been argued, is the end product, the cultural achievement of the "middle course." But those flying the middle course, as the shrewd and guilty Daedalus did, can never feel or know what Icarus felt and knew. The civic order promises and insists upon sustainability. The puer asks: sustainable for what? What is the point of being sustained for a long lifetime, of being sustained for eternity for that matter, if there can be no arrival in the Golden World?

Without a care for the consequences, Icarus flew up toward heaven.

# 8

# BEYOND BROKEN BOYS
*Heeding the Taunts of Perdix*

BEFORE ICARUS, DAEDALUS had a boy who was all he could have wanted. His sister had put under his tutelage her son Perdix, who was bright and gifted and full of life. Because Perdix's talent rivaled his own, Daedalus could not bear it: that his gift, his achievements were held by a spirited boy. The meanness of Daedalus's attempt to murder Perdix was appalling to the gods, and the falling boy's spirit was transmuted by Athena into a partridge. Later, as Daedalus grieved over the spent body of Icarus, the partridge taunted him from a bush.

Attempts to kill the puer spirit are always avenged, always answered. The substance of the taunts changes with cultural circumstances, but the message is always the same: *see what you've done, look what you've lost*. From within the civil order the taunts of Perdix seem unwarranted and capricious. Why hector a grieving father at such a moment? He is a hardworking and useful man. He had advised a life-preserving middle course for his lost son, and this sound advice was unheeded. Why taunt a man who works and who knows how to make things work?

Perdix and, of course, the gods know the answer. The workingman and his works are killers. They would kill the puer spirit itself if they could. Moreover, if they are as shrewd and industrious as Daedalus, they will appear to get away with it, they will thrive. The civil order they create and serve will honor them.

In this civil order the machines, including the deadliest, most infernal machines, work. Those who contract for them and use them prosper abundantly. But the taunts of Perdix are full of contempt for such marvels. They answer great industrial and technological revolutions with refusals and insults. They cry out to all youth who will hear: *don't conform, don't join, don't grow up.* They urge the most flamboyant denials of the civic order's conventions of speech, dress, appearance, and behavior. If the civic order prescribes disciplining the mind, they invite the young to blow their minds. If the civic order wants to make war, they urge making love instead. The taunts of Perdix are relentless, and their aim is sure. Whatever the civic order treasures, whatever it can't seem to live without, they revile that, refuse that. The taunts of Perdix take the part of the terrorists, whether alien or domestic. Produce a new technological wonder, and Perdix will work to implant a virus in it. Cure or contain a disease, and he will taunt you with an unthinkable new one.

The taunts of Perdix are neither civil nor nice. Our disinclination to hear them makes perfect sense, or at least common sense. But here common sense is the problem. Common sense is by its very nature culture bound. Common sense is willing to entertain a bit of the charm and lilt of boy-spirit but dreads coming to terms with the whole story. Common sense wants to keep the spark of the puer, but also to train and tame and educate it to the needs of the civic order. Common sense does not want the puer to perish, to crash and burn like Icarus, nor does it want the Icaruses of the world to have their impervious, headstrong way. Thus we have arrived at contemporary society's sincere, hand-wringing concern about inassimilable, incompletely realized, hazardous, and lost boys.

Contemporary culture has lost touch with its children, and as a result children are experienced as a proliferation of "problems." The continuing stream of journalistic and analytic attention to perceived crises in children's health, learning, and viability intensifies rather than clears the fog. This is because the apparent attention is not really focused on children—that is, on individual beings with distinctive natures—but on the inconvenience, difficulty, or threat children pose to civil order. To commerce, children are a promising and readily manipulated market. To an educational complex dedicated to the maintenance of its established assumptions and protocols, children present a collective bundle of underachievement, disabilities, and behavioral management challenges. Medical and therapeutic establishments identify a bewildering profusion of new pathologies in children: rampant, lethal allergies, attention deficits, and hyperactivity that must be treated with powerful psychoactive drugs. More and more children are reported to suffer from autism and Asperger's syndrome, pathologies in which children appear unable to feel what others feel and to respond to them appropriately. Children are found to be profoundly susceptible to debilitating conditions formerly confined to adults, including addictions, severe depression, and suicide. Millions of children are lost to the world, transfixed before video or computer screens for most of their unassigned waking hours. Children give up their personal identities to groups and gangs. Children are in danger of being hurt or killed, of hurting and killing others.

In such a culture, the remedies are as problematic as the pathologies and dysfunctions they set out to remediate. Parents obsessed over their children's potential failure to gain impressive college admission pay hundreds of thousands of dollars for special tuition, test preparation, and college brokerage. They are called soccer moms and helicopter parents, providing and demanding too much of everything for children already overstocked with possessions and privileges and unnaturally buffered from developmentally necessary disappointments and losses. At the same time there are legions of "latch-key" children who are unstimulated, unsupervised, and otherwise uncared for by working or otherwise preoccupied parents.

As for pathology, suspicions mount that medicines are cause, not cure. Perhaps required inoculations cause autism. Perhaps antidepressants stimulate suicidal thinking. Perhaps the attention deficit prescriptions are medicating not a boyhood pathology but boyhood itself. Does a lack of scholastic rigor "leave children behind?" Or do we do children worse harm by hurrying them along? Is the school year long enough? Have we lost the pastoral ease and occasions for inventive play children experienced when school ended sooner and started later?

It is unlikely that a thoughtful reader of this book—and certainly any parent—has proceeded this far and not asked *so what can be done?* Surely there must be an alternative for a spirited boy other than lifelong imposture or death! Again, the problem here is common sense, which after all is no more than an accretion of habits and assumptions so deeply ingrained that we no longer think *about* them but rather *with* them. Common sense tells us the boy—his nature and nurture—must be improved and changed. But what if that can and will never happen? What if boy spirit is given and immutable? What if it is the prevailing culture and its common sense that must be changed? Could that be what Perdix is taunting us about?

Perhaps more than therapies and self-help schemes we need an unflinching *witness* to boy-spirit as it is, including an acknowledgment of its beauty, its saving gift in lightening and energizing our lives. To acknowledge the existential *value* of the puer is the first step in realizing the tragic enormity of snuffing it out. Such witness opens up a crucial possibility: that perhaps the problem lies in a culture not fit for children. What might transpire, what might happen to boys and girls in a culture that values what is sacred and beautiful in children's lives for what is, and not for its use? To raise such questions and to resist the old answers is the beginning of uncommon sense. It is the beginning of cultural transformation. It begins not with outrage, fiery reforms, or clear maps to a better way; it begins with clear, loving witness to what is inviolable and saving in children.

To understand and appreciate children, to love them, and to help them make their imaginative and practical way, we must willfully suspend anything like certainty that we know what children are like and how they are supposed to think and behave. We must put aside, if not abandon outright, our most cherished notions of child development, of stages and phases. Our allegiance must be to children, not to conceptual models, tests, and norms. Even more important is a willingness to reconsider what constitutes *data* about children, especially if that term is regarded scientifically, as in measurable, replicable units of something or other. Reducing childhood experience to that kind of data contributes to the fog we are trying to dispel.

Here one might well ask: What have we got then? This is what we've got. We have a loving disposition to actual, particular children, we have memory, and we have a treasure trove of stories. These are necessary but perhaps not sufficient conditions for understanding and appreciating children. There is also a biblical injunction to do something very basic and humbling—to *become* as little children. Perhaps the surrender of assumptions suggested above will, if it is a real surrender, amount to the same thing.

Memory is crucial to accessing childhood, and memory is gendered. As a man, my consideration of childhood has taken me to boyhood where, in our era, all is far from well. Was it ever thus? No, it was not. Great and enduring stories remind us that boys once made rapt progress through beckoning worlds, worlds worth exploring, however perilous the way ahead. Memory, if we dare, will do the same.

Boy spirit is not understood through analysis but through witness. The first impression is more feeling tone than describable quality. We sense a spark, something infectious in a boy's urge to get up and out and away. He wants to move. He wants to touch it, hold it, grab it, put it together, build it up, knock it down. He wants to make it move, get inside it, drive it, fly it away. He loves the look of it, the feel of it, the noise of it. He wants to take it outside, take you with him. He wants to show you, wants you to watch him. Maybe, for a minute, he wants you to help him. He wants to be amazed. He wants you to be amazed. He wants to run off, and he wants you to chase after him. He wants to get away, and he wants you to catch him. He wants to do it again.

He loves that you love him, and that is how he begins to love. In this he is irresistible. He is outraged but not cowed by meanness, neglect, and injury. He is neither aware of nor grateful for safety and comfort, but he thrives in them. Safety and comfort are the beginning of his understanding of home, of glad return. If he has been sufficiently loved and safe, if he knows home and loves home, he will play the hero and then one day possibly be a hero, a protector of loved ones, a savior of the city. He may also, even if he is safe and loved, play other parts. He may play villain or fool or rascal or wizard, but if he has been safe and loved, he will hold the hero above the rest.

He does not have to be taught place or how to feel about place. He is born prepared. His senses and his heart are keenly receptive to the imprint of places. Here you can serve. Take him outdoors, to parks, ponds, darkly canopied stands of trees, to streambeds studded with climbable rocks. Take him to the shore. Let him peer up into the faces of cliffs. From great heights let him gaze out over vast expanses. Hold him tight.

You cannot know and needn't bother about the thousands of place impressions that he will treasure and store when he is alone: the swirl of the wallpaper by the bed, the geometry of the dormered window, the pattern of tiles on the bathroom floor, the snow curled over the eaves, the creak of the stairs, the beckoning dark behind the furnace.

In pictures and in your travels, stand him in front of handsome structures: the classical court house, the cathedral, the castle, the imposing fortress. Let him behold the skyline of a great city. Tell him stories of great cities, great kingdoms. He already holds an intimation of such places and will store the images and stories in his deep knowing. He will go to animals, take their measure. Let him. Watch him watch them, squirrels, yard birds, rabbits, cats. Have a dog. Have two dogs.

Understand that he can lash out suddenly, that he can hit. Understand that he will throw things, drop things, break things on purpose. He can push. He can knock down. He can snatch what he knows is not his, hide and hoard it. Understand these things. Feel them as he is feeling them. Remember feeling them. Then correct him. Then stop him. In time he may feel a helpless longing to set fires, to shoot, to stab, to pierce, to blow things up. You must acknowledge these urges, too, perhaps remember them. Then instruct and correct. When you must, stay his hand, tell him no.

As soon as he can, he will turn his imagination and longing to remote times. He is equally charmed by the deep past and the deep future. He seems always to have known that there was a time of dinosaurs. Dark forests and remote jungles are equally familiar. Just as readily he will extend himself into the future, outer space, worlds beyond worlds.

He will be drawn to the trappings and the clothes of prior eras: the knight's armor, Robin Hood's tunic and tights, the pirate's buckled shoes, the tricorn hat, the cape, the sword, the bow and arrow, the chaps, the spurs, the six-guns. These dreams will flow seamlessly into dreams of sport, of colossal work. He will be enchanted first by the uniforms and equipment, tools and vehicles. He will treasure, then scatter and forget hats, helmets, balls, mitts, clubs, bats, rods, reels, skis, goggles, fins. He will mount and ride anything that moves. He will quickly learn to steer but not to slow or stop. He does not love the big machines but wonders how to reduce them to his size.

He is responsive to music, even when he seems oblivious. He can feel music carrying him. He will mouth the words without regard to their sense but feeling their attitude. In music he will sense crisis, sweetness, danger, love's longing and its loss. He will rise at once to making music, to the instruments, their burnished wood and gleaming brass, the thrilling complexity of stops and valves and felts and hammers. He moves at once to percussion.

He will enter stories earlier than you think, even as he fidgets, looks away, squirms off your lap. You must understand he *enters* the story long before he follows its sense. He enters the characters and the creatures. He enters the colors and the shapes. He is able to make them pulse with his own feeling. Show him, read him, tell him stories. When he has sufficient language to follow a story's sense, some stories will hold him fast, confirm him. Grimm tales of abandoned or imperiled children who make their way will do this almost certainly. Stories of the destined, miraculous birth will do this, stories of Moses in the bulrushes, Romulus and Remus, Jesus in the manger. Do not interpret or explain his stories. Do not tell him the moral of stories. He has already gone deeper than that. He has lived in those stories, and there is every chance that he will go on telling the story because it is now the story of himself.

He enters stories before he reads. Reading does not unlock stories or open them up. Reading is only the medium for accessing stories in texts. Reading, even facile reading, can deaden stories, even as the reader is carried along in the act. The effort and awareness of reading will begin to form a barrier, distancing the boy from the world in the story, so that in time he will be able to say and begin even to believe that it is only a story.

A boy's experience of other people, of his parents, siblings, adults, and other children compose his first stories. Before he enters texts, he enters *them*. He does not come to know them as he learns their names and qualities. He enters into them, absorbs them before he names and categorizes them. In this he is utterly indiscriminate. If he is safe and loved, he will enter, know, and love others eagerly. He will observe, he will wait before touching, before imposing. He will play alongside, listening, watching. Then he will risk offering a gesture, an exchange. He will follow or he will lead. He will do what the others are doing. He will play. He plays long before he is "taught" to play; he is not taught to play.

Boys who are loved and safe, boys who are witnessed rather than guided and shaped, are neither fearful nor fearsome. Such boys enter an open world, a story with all the elements, including loss, danger, evil, and death.

By contrast, in a culture in which children are really neither safe nor loved, where they are shaped and guided and lavishly provided for but insufficiently witnessed, danger lies everywhere. It lies in the coloring of apples. It lies in peanuts and in bees. It lies in fiberglass and household cleansers. It lies in competitive sports, in hurtful toddler games like musical chairs, in sadistic playground games like dodgeball. It lies in animal fat, in milk, in new strains of bacteria, in viruses, in the medicines devised to treat the viruses.

One cannot—and should not!—say with certainty how the world will look, how conditions will improve, what fears will be dispelled and what errors will be corrected once we regain an understanding and appreciation of children. To do so would be to set up as if one had figured it out, drawn closure, adjusted the engine, patched up the infrastructure. That is the last thing children need.

Whether born of arrogance or desperation, the assumption of certain knowledge about children and what is good for them is the heart of the problem. There is no such certainty, no such knowledge. Every boy, if he is safe and loved, is a work in progress. If he is lovingly and appreciatively witnessed, he is very likely to emerge a surprise, possibly a pleasant surprise, perhaps the last thing you expected. Hedged in by knowing expectations of what he is like, of how and what and how fast he should learn, of how he should behave, whom he should love, and what kind of work he should do, he will refuse in the now familiar ways: he will draw inward, act out crazily, rebel, get sick.

The taunts of Perdix can be abrading, deafening. No one can bear to hear them for long. It is easy to cheer for their suppression, to want to shut them up. We take pains to distance ourselves from them, take up residence elsewhere.

But turning away, while it may temporarily ease the mind, is not finally the answer. To stop our ears to the taunts of Perdix is to participate willfully in the normative non-seeing discussed above. To ease the mind or calm the nerves in this manner is to deny the source of the trouble. Perdix is not the problem; he has a complaint. The taunts of Perdix could save us, if they are understood as a witness to what really happened to the puer spirit and what that spirit reveals to us of the Golden World. The spiritually saving solution is not to turn away from anything that is insistent and true.

Because we cannot nurture viable children with certainties does not mean we cannot nurture them. It is disposition, not certainty, that is required. The basic dispositions have already been named: the disposition to love, to appreciate, to witness. When these dispositions are central and uncompromised, they are more than capable of resisting seemingly enormous cultural pressures to nurture and school children otherwise. Rightly disposed parents, joining will to instinct, have always done this, but because this disposition is by its nature unformulaic and fluid, there has been no movement or theory or school to carry it forth.

The first condition sought by the loving parental disposition is safety, and this cannot be overemphasized. Abraham Maslow rightly put a child's safety at the foundation of any possible future realization. This is real safety, the soul's apprehension of safety. It cannot be materially produced. It cannot be abstracted to suburban or rural refuges. It certainly cannot be gated. No privilege can buy it. A child can be safe and loved in a tenement or in a trailer park. Children who live in unworldly opulence, with every toy and diversion, can and do live in hellish anxiety and fear.

A loving disposition can stand guard against and resolutely refuse to practice what the angry Scottish psychiatrist R. D. Laing called psychic robbery. Psychic robbery is the practice of substituting one's own desires for what a child is thinking and feeling. Psychic robbery occurs in seemingly benign ways, as when a child declares, "I hate broccoli," and a parent responds, "You don't hate broccoli." It also occurs—normatively—when children express their darkest and most intense feelings: "I hate baby," "I want to *kill* you." When parents and other nurturers answer "No you don't," "You don't feel that way," the child is not reassured; he is made anxious and hurried into despair, because the truth has not been acknowledged.

Psychic robbery is exponentially worse than disagreement. A child's dark or challenging declaration can be met with sheer witness, with questions, with consolation, or with objection, but if it is met with a knowing, manipulative, or perhaps angry insistence that his feeling is not felt, that what was actually felt is an alien mental state, that is the beginning of a child's profoundest anxiety and despair. The child is easily cowed into verbal denials and recantations, but the underlying and now inaccessible interior condition is deepening anxiety and despair. To deny and replace any true mental state felt or declared by a child is in effect to negate him, to cut him off from connectedness to others, to undermine his safety. Children detached in this way do not forsake the dark or unwanted sentiment. To the contrary, because the sentiment has been unwitnessed and unmet, it will become a fixation. Only in a detached, unreachable condition can a child live on in a world of psychic robbers. He will not relate to or find himself in seemingly well-intentioned but actually frightened classrooms and school curricula where the dark thought is unutterable on pain of expulsion, where it cannot be found in the assigned texts or even in the libraries, where organized exercises to identify and express "feelings" are highly manipulative, transparent attempts to lighten and sweeten the real thing—not to open it up, but to seal it off. There is ultimately no denying the darkness. Psychic robbery is both a selfish and futile practice. It is generated by a fearful disposition, not a loving one. The culture in which psychic robbery is normative will find itself overwhelmed by the very terror it refuses to witness in children.

It is by no means certain but perhaps very promising that in addition to a loving disposition to children, certain pathways ahead do beckon brightly—in fact, have always beckoned brightly. Again, my experience limits me here to the experience of boys. I believe boys can thrive. In the past some have thrived. We have their stories. Loved and safe as they begin, boys have and perhaps can again make their way vigorously through experiences both enlivening and self-affirmingly great. In this condition their lives unfold as in a story. The first is the story of boyhood itself, the limitless exuberance and danger and wonder of the puer spirit, the puer spirit played out in every way, in every place, with whatever kind of gear, and with whatever companions happen to be at hand.

The distinctive feature of the taunts of Perdix is that we can hear them. The taunters and their upsetting message are right out there, so to speak, in the civil order's face. They are a true witness, but the deeper truth is prior to any complaint. The deeper truth, all but consciously lost, is that there has been and there can still be an ecstatic spirit afoot and aloft in the world. It is the spirit of the puer, and it can be embodied. Such figures have moved among us. If pressed, we can remember them, perhaps remember being moved by them, being one of them. They could be our children.

# NOTES

## 1. THE EXPERIENCE OF BOYS

1. James Hillman, *A Blue Fire* (New York: Harper and Row, 1989), 228.
2. Erik Erikson, *Childhood and Society* (New York: Norton, 1985), 102–3.
3. Ibid., 255.

## 2. THE FIGURE OF ICARUS

1. Ovid, *Metamorphoses,* Loeb Classic Library edition, translated by Frank Justus Miller, rev. by G. P. Goold (Cambridge, Mass.: Harvard University Press, 1999), 2.34–37.
2. Ibid., 2.282–89.
3. Ibid., 2.328–29.
4. Ibid., 2.160–65.
5. Ibid., 8.224–27.
6. Ibid., 8.190–98.
7. Ibid., 8.199–204.
8. Ibid., 8.241–42.

## 3. THE EXILE OF DAEDALUS AND THE DAWN
## OF MODERN CONSCIOUSNESS

1. Ovid, *Metamorphoses,* 8.192–96.
2. Friedrich Nietzsche, *The Birth of Tragedy*: *Basic Writings of Nietzsche,* translated by Walter Kaufman (New York: Random House, 1968), 33.
3. Ibid., 35.
4. Ibid., 37.
5. Ibid., 40.
6. Ibid., 41.
7. Ibid., 23.
8. Ibid., 43.

9. Ibid., 47.

10. Ibid., 61.

11. Ibid., 61.

12. Ibid., 73.

13. Ibid., 74.

14. Plato, *The Republic,* translated by F. M. Cornford (New York: Oxford University Press, 1988), 2.377.

15. Ibid., 2.395.

16. Ibid., 3.413.

17. Ibid., 3.414.

18. Ibid., 3.399, 3.400.

19. Ibid., 2.378, 2.387.

20. Ibid., 3.397.

21. Nietzsche, *The Birth of Tragedy,* 92.

22. Peter Shaffer, *Equus* (New York: Penguin Books, 1985), act 1, p. 25.

23. Ibid., 1.7, p. 31.

24. Ibid., 1.21, p. 74.

25. Ibid., 1.35, p. 108.

## 4. ICARUS EMBODIED

1. Robert Payne, *Ancient Rome* (New York: American Heritage Press, 1970), 260.

## 5. ICARUS IN THE MODERN WORLD

1. Stacy Schiff, *Saint-Exupéry* (New York: DaCapo Press, 1994), 65–66.

2. Ibid., 76.

3. Ibid., 53.

4. Ibid., 53.

5. Ibid., 83.

6. Ibid., 141.

7. Ibid., 149.

8. Ibid., 150.

9. Ibid., 179.

10. Ibid., 182.

11. Ibid., 207.

12. Ibid., 225.

13. Ibid., 248.

14. Ibid., 431.

15. Ibid., 96.

16. Ibid., 98.

17. Ibid., 96.
18. Ibid., 254.
19. Consuelo Saint-Exupéry, *The Tale of the Rose,* translated by Esther Allen (New York: Random House, 2001), 19.
20. Ibid., 37–38.
21. Ibid., 77.
22. Ibid., 255.
23. Ibid., 221.
24. Ibid., 284.
25. Ibid., viii.
26. Antoine Saint-Exupéry, *The Little Prince,* translated by Richard Howard (Hong Kong: Harcourt, 2000), 1, 2.
27. Ibid., 64.
28. Ibid., 68.
29. Ibid., 83.
30. Antoine Saint-Exupéry, *Wind, Sand, and Stars,* translated by Lewis Gallautiére (New York: Harcourt, 1967), 11.

## 6. ICARUS OBSERVED FROM THE GROUND

1. W. H. Auden, *Collected Shorter Poems* (New York: Random House, 1964), 124.
2. Marie-Louise von Franz, *The Problem of the Puer Aeternis* (Toronto: Inner City Books, 2000), 7.
3. Ibid., 8.
4. Ibid., 9.
5. Ibid., 9.
6. Ibid., 20.
7. Ibid., 34–35.
8. Ibid., 35.
9. Ibid., 24.
10. Ibid., 84.

## 7. ICARUS AND THE GOLDEN WORLD

1. Robert Johnson, *Balancing Heaven and Earth* (San Francisco: HarperSanFrancisco, 1998), 11.
2. Ibid., 14.
3. Ibid., 15.
4. Kenneth Grahame, *The Wind in the Willows* (New York: Charles Scribner's Sons, 1981), 77.
5. Richard Hawley, *Seeing Things* (New York: Walker and Company, 1987), 46.
6. Ibid., 52.

# BIBLIOGRAPHY

Aeschylus. *The Oresteia*. Translated by Robert Fagles. New York: Penguin Books, 1979.

Auden, W. H. *Collected Shorter Poems*. New York: Random House, 1964.

Blake, William. *William Blake: The Illustrated Poets*. New York: Oxford University Press, 1986.

Calasso, Roberto. *The Marriage of Cadmus and Harmony*. New York: Alfred A. Knopf, 1993.

Carpenter, Humphrey. *Secret Gardens*. Boston: Houghton Mifflin, 1988.

Erikson, Erik. *Childhood and Society*. New York: Norton, 1985.

Grahame, Kenneth. *The Wind in the Willows*. New York: Charles Scribner's Sons, 1981.

Graves, Robert. *The Greek Myths*. London: The Folio Society, Ltd., 1996.

Hawley, Richard. *Seeing Things*. New York: Walker and Company, 1987.

Hillman, James. *A Blue Fire*. New York: Harper and Row, 1989.

———, ed. *Puer Papers*. Dallas: Spring Publications, 1994.

Johnson, Robert. *Balancing Heaven and Earth*. San Francisco: HarperSan Francisco, 1998.

———. *He*. King of Prussia, Penn.: Religious Publishing Co., 1974.

*The New English Bible*. Oxford: Oxford University Press, 1970.

Nietzsche, Friedrich. *The Birth of Tragedy*: *Basic Writings of Nietzsche*. Translated by Walter Kaufman. New York: Random House, 1968.

Ovid. *Metamorphoses*. Translated by A. D. Melville. New York: Oxford University Press, 1986.

———. *Metamorphoses.* Translated by Frank Justus Miller. Cambridge: Harvard University Press, 1999.

———. *The Art of Love.* Translated by J. H. Mozley. Cambridge: Harvard University Press, 1985.

Payne, Robert. *Ancient Rome.* New York: American Heritage Press, 1970.

Plato. *The Apology: The Last Days of Socrates.* Translated by Hugh Tredennick. New York: Penguin Books, 1970.

———. *Euthyphro: The Last Days of Socrates.* Translated by Hugh Tredennick. New York: Penguin Books, 1970.

———. *The Republic.* Translated by F. M. Cornford. New York: Oxford University Press, 1988.

Robinson, C. E. *Hellas.* Boston: Beacon Press, 1955.

Saint-Exupéry, Antoine. *The Little Prince.* Translated by Richard Howard. Hong Kong: Harcourt, 2000.

———. *Night Flight.* Translated by Stuart Gilbert. New York: Harcourt, 1932.

———. *Wind, Sand, and Stars.* Translated by Lewis Gallautiére. New York: Harcourt, 1967.

Saint-Exupéry, Consuelo. *The Tale of the Rose.* Translated by Esther Allen. New York: Random House, 2001.

Schiff, Stacy. *Saint-Exupéry.* New York: DaCapo Press, 1994.

Shaffer, Peter. *Equus.* New York: Penguin Books, 1985.

Sophocles. *Oedipus the King.* Translated by Bernard Knox. New York: Pocket Books, 1994.

von Franz, Marie-Louise. *The Problem of the Puer Aeternis.* Toronto: Inner City Books, 2000.

Weston, Jessie L. *The Legend of Sir Perceval.* London: AMS, 1972.

# INDEX